The 500
BEST-VALUE
WINES *in the* LCBO

⧼2015⧽

The 500 BEST-VALUE WINES *in the* LCBO

∽ 2015 ∾

{ THE DEFINITIVE GUIDE
TO THE BEST WINE DEALS
IN THE LIQUOR CONTROL
BOARD OF ONTARIO }

Rod Phillips

UPDATED SEVENTH EDITION

whitecap

Copyright © 2014 by Rod Phillips
Whitecap Books
First edition 2007. Seventh edition 2014.

EDITED BY Patrick Geraghty
INTERIOR DESIGN BY Grace Partridge
COVER DESIGN BY Grace Partridge and Andrew Bagatella
TYPESET BY Champagne Choquer
PROOFREAD BY Kaitlyn Till

Printed in Canada

❧

Cataloguing data available from Library and Archives Canada.

ISBN: 978-1-77050-241-3

The publisher acknowledges the financial support of the Government of
Canada through the Canada Book Fund (CBF) and the Province of British
Columbia through the Book Publishing Tax Credit.

20 19 18 17 16 15 14   1 2 3 4 5 6 7

CONTENTS

The Reds

PREFACE TO THE 2015 EDITION

This book is a guide to the best-value wines within the wide range available in LCBO (Liquor Control Board of Ontario) stores throughout Ontario. (And if you're not in Ontario, chances are that you'll find many of these wines available where you live.) There are so many good- to great-value wines available at reasonable prices in the LCBO, and it's a pity not to take advantage of them. If you tend to buy the same few wines time after time, this list will help you broaden your horizons and reduce the financial risk in being adventurous. If you're already adventurous, you're sure to find wines here that you haven't tried.

To compile this list of 500 wines, I tasted nearly all the wines continuously available in the LCBO, and my ratings and reviews point you to wine values and styles you'll easily recognize. Each wine is ranked out of five stars (see How I Rate the Wines on page 5), but I encourage you to read the description of each wine. Stars (like ratings on a 100-point scale) don't tell you what any wine is like when you drink it, nor do they tell you if you'll like the wine.

I hope you find this book a useful guide to discovering wines you enjoy. If you come across a wine that's not listed here but that you think should be included in the next edition, please let me know. You can reach me at rodphillips@worldsofwine.com.

Cheers!

THANKS

Once again, I thank all the wine agencies and individual wineries, together with their sales, communications and marketing people, for providing the wines I tasted for this book.

I also wish to thank the Liquor Control Board of Ontario for inviting me to the regular tastings of Vintages, Vintages Essentials and General Purchase wines.

Again, it was a pleasure to work with the people at Whitecap Books: Andrew Bagatella, Champagne Choquer, Michelle Furbacher, Patrick Geraghty, Steph Hill, Jesse Marchand and Kaitlyn Till.

WHAT'S NEW IN THE 2015 EDITION

This edition includes many new wines that have appeared on the LCBO's shelves in the last year. Some new styles of wine have emerged, and some regions have increased their representation. Changes like these are reflected in the range of wines reviewed here. There are over 100 new wines in this edition, with the biggest changes occurring in French white wines and French, Italian and Ontario red wines.

But many of the wines here are veterans that have been in the LCBO for years. This is not a bad thing, as most of them stay on the shelves because they're good wines, reliable vintage after vintage and consistently supported by consumers. After re-tasting almost the whole LCBO inventory, I dropped some of these wines, added others and changed some ratings. Although most LCBO wines do not vary much from vintage to vintage, some do, and I've made some changes accordingly.

Since I tasted for the last edition, the prices of many wines have increased, quite a few by a dollar or more. This has meant recalibrating the meaning of "value" in some cases. Is a wine I rated four stars in the 2014 edition, when it cost $12.95, still worth four stars when it costs $14.95? Given that the general trend is toward higher prices, I have made only a few adjustments of this sort.

Overall, the quality of wines in the LCBO has been rising steadily. The first edition of this book, published in 2008, included wines rated from three to five stars. By the 2011 edition, there were very few three-star wines. In this edition, as in the previous one, there are none. That indicates a steady rise in quality and value. There's just no need to buy mediocre and poor-value wines.

SOME WINE TRENDS TO WATCH FOR

Tasting almost all the wines in the LCBO has alerted me to a number of trends.

Argentine malbec continues its roll, but there's still a lot of speculation about "The Next Big Red." Could it be bonarda (also from Argentina; see page 103 for one in this edition), syrah (rather than shiraz), or tempranillo (Spain's signature variety, now planted in many parts of the world)? Maybe pinotage (from South Africa)? Maybe none of these. The preconditions for going big are: there has to be plenty of it (all four of the above qualify), it has to be made in a popular style (all can be) and it has to catch on (we'll see).

Rosé wines continue to increase in number and popularity. The new breed of varietally-labelled rosés tend to be dry and well made, but look for well-made off-dry styles, too. Starting in spring, the LCBO brings in "seasonal volumes" of rosés that aren't available year round, but I think there's enough demand to justify a much better year-round selection.

Sparkling wine is finally escaping from the celebration ghetto. People have realized that sparkling wine (including champagne) is not only for anniversaries, weddings, birthdays and the like, but for everyday drinking as well. As a result, there are more and more sparkling wines available, as the range in this book shows.

"Regionality" is still a buzz word. Wine-producing countries like Australia and Chile want us to think in regional, not simply national, terms. They want us to go looking for a wine from South Australia, Barossa Valley or Margaret River, not just for "an Australian wine." In this year's list you'll see more and more wines labelled by specific and smaller regions, like Langhorne Creek (Australia), Limarí Valley (Chile), and Santa Ynez Valley (California).

The LCBO has abandoned its ventures into wine packaged in plastic bottles and Tetra Pak cartons. Glass has won, but the LCBO now mandates a maximum weight for bottles in order to prevent a tendency of putting wines into heavy bottles so that they might seem weightier in quality. Lighter bottles save energy in transportation and are easier on the backs of LCBO workers.

Alcohol levels in wine continue their gentle rise, with levels of 14 percent and 14.5 percent becoming more common. Although there are some complaints about this, and scattered attempts to bring alcohol levels down, there's no evidence that levels are declining.

HOW I DESCRIBE THE WINES

The most common way of describing wines in North America is to use fruit, spices and other produce (and things) as references. We've all seen wines described as having aromas and flavours like "red cherry, plum and black pepper, with notes of leather" or "tropical fruit, peach and citrus." I call these "Carmen Miranda" reviews. (She was the Brazilian singer famous for her hats covered with exotic fruit.) Sometimes reviewers get even more specific and find flavours such as "damson plum, ripe Red Delicious apples and Bing cherries, with nuances of finely-ground green peppercorns."

Very few people can distinguish these flavours in wine, although it's a skill that many can learn. But even though it is possible to discern these aromas and flavours, no wine ever really tastes primarily like a combination of cherry, plum and black pepper (just imagine it), or of tropical fruit, peach and citrus. (You're better off drinking fruit juice, if that's what you're looking for.) There might be hints or reminders of these flavours in the wine, but they're details. Just watch professionals swirling and sniffing (sometimes favouring one nostril over the other) as they strain to pick up and identify the most subtle and fleeting aromas. Focusing on these nuances misses the big picture.

In this book I focus on the main characteristics of each wine and on its style: Is it light, medium or full bodied? Is it simple and fruity or well structured? Is it dry, off-dry, sweet or very sweet? Is it tannic or not? Does it have a smooth, tangy, juicy or crisp texture? These are the most important qualities of any wine whether you're looking for a wine to sip on its own or one to go with specific food.

Most of us describe wine in these terms. We say we like red wine that's full bodied and rich, white wine that's light and refreshing or rosé that's slightly sweet. When we're looking for wine to go with dinner, we might think of a heavy red for steak or a lighter white or crisp rosé for a summer salad.

What we don't look for is a wine with flavours of black plums or raspberries, or notes of red grapefruit, black pepper or honey. And we certainly don't say we love wines with flavours of wet stones, smoky tar or hard-ridden horses—the sort of descriptions loved by some wine reviewers.

In short, you'll find that the reviews in this book describe wines in the common-sense way in which most people think of them.

THE LCBO'S SWEETNESS SCALE

The LCBO provides a convenient sweetness indicator for each wine, telling you where the wine sits on a spectrum from extra dry to sweet. The LCBO used to indicate only the actual sugar levels in wine (in grams per litre), but the current system is much more useful because it indicates how sweet the wine seems, regardless of the amount of sugar in it. That's really important, because sugar can be counteracted by acidity; if you taste two wines with the same level of sugar, the one with more acidity will taste less sweet than the one with less acidity.

The LCBO's "perceived sweetness" system is coded like this, and these are the letters you'll see for each wine in this book:

X D = Extra Dry: No perceived sweetness; clean, crisp acidic finish

D = Dry: No distinct sweetness; well-rounded, balanced acidity

M = Medium: Slight sweetness perceived

M S = Medium Sweet: Noticeably sweet

S = Sweet: Distinctly sweet

For example, most cabernet sauvignons and pinot noirs are **X D** and most chardonnays and pinot grigios are **D**, but icewines, of course, are **S**. Nearly all the wines in this book are **X D** or **D**. In a few cases for which the LCBO website doesn't show the perceived sweetness, I've given my own rating after tasting the wine.

If you still want to know the actual sugar level—as some people do for health reasons—it's shown for each wine on the LCBO's website.

HOW I RATE THE WINES

I tasted not only all the wines listed in this book, but about another thousand available in the LCBO General Purchase and Vintages Essentials lists. As far as I know, I'm the only person who tastes almost all LCBO wines in a short period (I do it in five weeks), and this gives me a unique perspective on them.

I taste the reds at a cool temperature—the way they should be served—and the whites, rosés and sparkling wines chilled, but not cold.

The 500 wines in this book are the ones I consider the best in terms of their intrinsic quality and value. The quality of a wine depends on the balance among its various components (fruit, acidity, alcohol and tannins) and the complexity of its flavours, structure and texture. A wine that's well balanced and very complex scores higher than one with little complexity or poor balance.

All the wines here are good-to-excellent quality, and the five-star rating reflects their value to the consumer. A $10 wine rated four-and-a-half stars is better value than a $10 wine rated three-and-a-half stars. But good value can be found at all price levels. A $30 wine rated four stars has a quality level that is very good value for its price.

Here's what my star system means:

★ ★ ★ ★ ★   It's hard to imagine better value at this price. This wine is very well balanced and very complex.

★ ★ ★ ★ ½   Excellent value at this price. The wine is well balanced and very complex.

★ ★ ★ ★   Very good value at this price. The wine is well balanced and complex.

★ ★ ★ ½   Above-average value at this price. The wine has fair levels of balance and complexity.

★ ★ ★   Good value at this price. The wine is well made but might be a little unbalanced and might lack much complexity.

HOW TO READ MY REVIEWS

Indicates that the wine is new to this edition.

BRAND OR WINERY

RATING (*out of five*)

GRAPE VARIETY

VINTAGE YEAR

NEW!
★ ★ ★ ★

La Mascota Cabernet Sauvignon 2011

MENDOZA $14.40 (292110) **D**

Argentina produces many fine cabernet sauvignons, which go as well with the country's beef-heavy diet as the better-known malbecs. This full-bodied cabernet is quite rich, with plush and concentrated flavours and a generous and smooth texture. It has enough acidity to suit it to food, though, and it's a natural for well-seasoned red meats.

NOTES

[Vintages Essential] *indicates the wine is found in the Vintages section, or at a Vintages store.* [Non-vintage] *indicates that the wine doesn't show a year on its label.*

LCBO PRODUCT CODE

LCBO SWEETNESS INDICATOR

REGION

PRICE
(*per 750 mL bottle, unless otherwise indicated*)

ABOUT THE LCBO

The LCBO (including Vintages, its fine-wine arm) sells more than 80 percent of the wine purchased in Ontario, and its wine sales total more than $1.6 billion a year. The remaining wine sales are made by winery retail stores, online merchants and importing agents who sell directly to restaurants, bars and individual clients. The LCBO is where most Ontarians shop for wine because it has so many locations and offers the biggest range of imported and Canadian wine in the province.

Critics of the LCBO often complain that its wine selection is too limited, but most consumers find it bewilderingly large. That's the reason for this book. It guides you to the best-value wines on the General Purchase List, which comprises most of the wines in the LCBO. The others are in Vintages stores or Vintages sections of the LCBO. I review some of the wines continuously available in the Vintages Essentials collection, which numbers about 100.

It can sometimes be a challenge to locate a particular wine in the LCBO. There are 630 LCBO stores throughout the province, plus more than 200 small agencies in isolated localities, and the range of wine varies widely from outlet to outlet. The main LCBO stores in major cities carry nearly all the LCBO's wines, while others have a more limited selection on hand.

In the unlikely event that you forget to bring this book along when you go wine shopping, you can ask an LCBO Product Consultant for help. They have passed LCBO wine-knowledge exams and they know the LCBO's inventory well.

If you see a wine in this book that you'd like to try but you discover it's not in your local LCBO, call the liquor board's helpline at 1-800-ONT-LCBO (1-800-668-5226). An agent will tell you the nearest store that has the wine you're looking for. Alternatively, use the search engine at www.lcbo.com to find a wine and identify the LCBO stores close to you that have it.

Bear in mind that the LCBO's inventory is constantly changing. New wines are added and others are dropped. Prices change, too, according to currency exchange fluctuations and other factors. The prices in this book were correct when it went to press.

The vintages of wines in the LCBO also change, as one vintage sells out and is replaced by the next. You might see a 2011 wine listed here and find that the 2012 vintage is on the LCBO shelf. For the most part, the vintages in the wines on the General Purchase List have relatively little variation, and it's safe to go with my reviews and ratings even when the vintage is different.

BUYING, SERVING & DRINKING WINE: SOME COMMON QUESTIONS

Are wines sealed with a screw cap poorer quality than wines sealed with a cork?
Not at all. In fact, some of the best-known and most reliable producers,
like Wolf Blass and Peter Lehmann in Australia, seal all their still wines,
including their top brands, with screw caps. There's some scattered debate
about the use of screw caps on wines intended for long-term aging, but
there's no doubt at all that they are excellent for wines meant to be drunk
within five or six years of being made—like all the wines in this book.
Natural corks can contain bacteria capable of mildly or seriously tainting
wine. They can also produce variability from bottle to bottle, whereas
wines sealed with screw caps are almost always more consistent. Are screw
caps the last word in wine-bottle closures? Probably not, as experiments
are ongoing with other types of seals.

Are wines in boxes and plastic bottles poorer quality than wines in glass bottles?
There's a common misconception that only inferior wine is sold in boxes
(like Tetra Pak cartons) or bottles made of plastic (such as PET, a food-
grade plastic that does not taint the contents). You can't generalize about
the quality of wine based on its packaging; after all, there are plenty of
poor wines in glass bottles. In practice, though, many producers put their
lower-quality wines in boxes and plastic. The only reason excellent wine
might not be sold in such packaging is that there's some question about
how long it preserves wine in good condition.

Are more expensive wines better than cheaper ones?
In very broad terms, there is often a relationship between quality and
price. High-quality wine demands high-quality grapes (which are often
more expensive to grow or buy) and may involve more expenses in
production, such as the use of oak barrels. But although it's not as easy to
find a great wine under $10 or $15 as over $20 or $30, this book shows that
there are plenty of high-quality wines at very reasonable prices.

Should I worry about the alcohol level in wine?
By definition, wine contains alcohol. Nearly all of us buy wine not only
because we enjoy the flavour and texture, but also for the effects of the
alcohol. That said, the level of alcohol—which must be shown on the

bottle and is expressed as a percentage by volume—varies widely. Some whites, like off-dry rieslings, have about 10 percent alcohol, while some reds, notably zinfandels, exceed 14.5 percent. The difference is significant: A glass of 14.5-percent-alcohol wine gives you almost 50 percent more alcohol than the same glass of 10-percent-alcohol wine. But the difference between 13.5 and a 14.5 percent wine is quite small. Whether alcohol level is important depends on the circumstances—for example, how important it is for you to remain alert and unimpaired. As far as your experience of the wine is concerned, high alcohol is not a problem as long as the wine is balanced. If the wine smells of alcohol or if you can feel the warmth of the alcohol as you drink it, it's unbalanced and the wine is flawed, just as it is when the acidity dominates the fruit or when jammy fruit kills the acidity and leaves the wine flat.

Are wine labels a good guide to what's inside the bottle?

Labels are an important part of marketing wine. Wine is no different from other products, and producers expect that consumers will often be drawn to a particular wine by its packaging—and that usually means the label. Labels can be sophisticated (like those on many expensive and ultra-premium wines), fun (like most of the labels featuring animals), and even provocative (like the Fat Bastard brand). The fact that all are represented in this book shows that there's no necessary link between the label and quality or value. But beyond projecting an image, labels provide consumers with important information. Depending on where the wine is from, the label tells the grape variety (or varieties) used to make the wine and/or where the grapes were grown. The label also tells you the vintage and the alcohol content, and it might give information such as whether the wine is organic, kosher or fair trade. Some of this information might be on a back label along with a description of the wine, the production process or the producer. But bear in mind that any description of the wine on the back label is written by the producer to promote sales.

Does the serving temperature of wine make any difference?

The serving temperature of wine matters a lot because it affects qualities in the wine such as flavour and texture (the way the wine feels in your mouth). Too many people (and restaurants) serve white wine too cold and red wine too warm. White wines are refreshing when they're chilled, but most should not be served straight from the fridge. Wine that's too cold has little flavour, so take white wine out of the fridge 15 or 20 minutes before you serve it. Red wine, on the other hand, should be served cooler than it usually is—especially in restaurants where the wine is stored on shelves in the dining room. Red wine should feel cool in your mouth, and that means cooler than the 20°C or higher of most homes and restaurants. (The guideline of serving red wine "at room temperature" is not very useful if you like to live in sauna-like temperatures.) If your red wine is too warm, it will feel coarse and flabby and won't have the refreshing quality that makes wine such an ideal partner for food. To cool red wine that's too warm, put it in the fridge for 15 or 20 minutes before serving. Remember, it's better to serve any wine too cool than too warm; it will warm up quite quickly in your glass.

How many different kinds of wine glasses do I need?

If you look in wine accessory, kitchen and even many department stores, you'll see a wide selection of wine glasses in many different shapes and sizes, often classified by grape variety. Do you really need one glass for chardonnay, another for merlot and another for shiraz? No, you don't. Although the shape and size of the glass can sometimes highlight the qualities in different wines, you can enjoy nearly all from one or two different glasses. In general, most people prefer to drink wine from finer glasses than from thicker-sided tumblers or glasses. Look for glasses that are wider toward the bottom of the bowl, and fill the glass only to the widest point. That gives room for the aromas to collect. And if you're interested in tasting wine as judges and professionals do, buy some tasting glasses at a wine accessories store. They're smaller than most wine glasses, wide at the bottom and tapered toward the mouth (like the stylized glasses on the cover of this book), and they bring out the aromas and flavours of wines very well. One style of wine often drunk from a specific glass is sparkling wine. It's frequently served in a tall, slender glass (called a flute) that shows off the bubbles to best effect, but many professionals prefer to drink sparkling wine from a bigger, wider glass.

Should I let wine "breathe" before I serve it?

There's a common belief that wine should be opened and left standing to "breathe" for an hour or two before being served. It's based on the theory, which is true, that most wine improves after being exposed to air for a short time. But simply opening a bottle of wine exposes a very small amount of wine (the dime-size surface in the neck of the bottle) to air, and it makes no perceptible difference to the wine. Pouring the wine into glasses as soon as you open the bottle exposes the wine to air far more effectively than letting it stand in the open bottle for hours. You can also decant wine to expose it to air, and that raises the question . . .

Do I need to decant wine?

There are two reasons to decant wine. The first is to pour the wine without disturbing the sediment that has collected in the bottom of the bottle to make sure it doesn't get into your glass. Of course, this is necessary only when there's sediment present, and that's rarely the case with wines made for early drinking, like virtually all the wines in this book. The second reason to decant does apply to the wines here—in fact, it applies to any wine, whether red, white or rosé—and that's to expose the wine to some air before you drink it. This is more accurately called "aerating" than "decanting," and it generally improves the aromas, flavours and texture of wine, and therefore its overall quality. You needn't buy an expensive decanter (there are many on the market for less than $15), but look for one with a broad mouth and a wide bottom. If you don't have a decanter at hand but want to aerate a bottle of wine, pour it into a clean bottle (or a pitcher) and then back into the original bottle once or twice.

What do I do with leftover wine?

Opened wine lasts longer if you keep it in the refrigerator and longer still if you minimize exposure to air. Just re-corking or screwing the cap back on a half-finished bottle leaves the wine exposed to a lot of air, so it's better to pour leftover wine into a smaller container, like a clean half-bottle, where there's little or no air between the surface of the wine and the top of the bottle. If you're keeping a half-full bottle, store it standing up, rather than on its side, so that the surface exposed to air is minimal. Kept in the fridge like this, leftover wine should be good for at least two or three days. If you have leftover sparkling wine, use the same re-sealer you'd use for a bottle of carbonated soft drink.

Does wine improve with age? Should I have a wine cellar?

While some wines are made for aging, the bulk of the world's wine is made for drinking as soon as it's released for sale. It will not improve with age; in fact, it will eventually deteriorate and become undrinkable. Most consumers buy wine as they need it, but there's no reason why you shouldn't keep a number of bottles of wine on hand for emergencies. For that purpose, you don't need a proper cellar with controlled temperature and humidity, but your wine will keep best if it's in a dark, cool place (ideally between 10°C and 15° C). The corner of a basement, a closet or the space under a staircase might be suitable, but a kitchen counter, where the wine will be exposed to light and heat, is not. Wine kept in too-warm conditions develops a "stewed" flavour. If you want to store a few dozen or more bottles of wine so they improve over a longer term, check the Internet or a wine accessories store for information on wine cabinets or how to build a wine cellar.

MATCHING WINE & FOOD

Matching food with wine is not nearly as difficult as many people think—or are led to think by too many wine professionals who make it sound like rocket science. Ignore the complicated treatises that tell you that a smoky note in the wine echoes a hint of smoke in a dish. Similarly, ignore the food and wine matching guides and apps that tell you to pair this food with that wine. Both food and wine vary widely—there's no one chicken curry and no one pinot gris—and you're better off following your own common sense.

That said, a few basic guidelines can help you choose a pairing that does what it should: enhance your enjoyment of both the food and the wine. What you most want to avoid is a pairing where one overwhelms or interferes with your enjoyment of the other. For example, a full-flavoured wine will smother food that has delicate flavours, and sweet food can make dry wines taste sour. The best pairing leaves the food tasting the way the cook intended and the wine the way the winemaker planned.

Matching wine and food should be fun. Each review in this book includes a food match that works well, but don't take them too literally. Each suggestion represents a style. A wine that goes with beef will almost always team equally well with lamb and other red meats, and one that pairs successfully with chicken will also marry happily with turkey.

Some basic guidelines:

- Match heavier dishes (like red meat and hearty meat or vegetable stews) with medium- to full-bodied wines and lighter dishes (like salads and white fish) with light- to medium-bodied wines. The weight of food often comes from sauces. White fish alone is light, but a cream sauce makes it heavier.

- Focus on the style of the entire dish, not just the main item. The overall flavour of unseasoned roast chicken is mild. But chicken in a spicy, rich tomato sauce has more complexity.

- Herbs and spices give richer and more complex texture to food. Barbecued pork has more complexity than unseasoned pork, for example, and a wine that pairs well with richly flavoured food will be a better match.

- Focus on the style of the wine, not only its colour. For the purpose of matching food, a full-bodied, rich, oaked chardonnay might have more in common with a red wine than with a light-bodied, delicate white.

ARGENTINA

ARGENTINA IS THE FIFTH-LARGEST wine producer in the world. It has only recently become a major wine exporter, but has quickly earned a reputation for producing quality wines at prices that offer very good value. Although better known for its red wines (especially malbec), Argentina produces many excellent whites. One of the most interesting white grapes is torrontés, which has become the country's signature white variety. It generally shows pungent aromas and a crisp, refreshing texture. Other whites are made from popular varieties like chardonnay and pinot grigio.

Most Argentine wine is labelled by the sprawling Mendoza region, although some is starting to be labelled by Mendoza's smaller sub-regions. Other important wine regions are San Juan, Salta/Cafayate in the north, and Patagonia in the south.

★ ★ ★ ★

FuZion 'Alta' Torrontés/Pinot Grigio 2013

MENDOZA $9.95   (168419) **XD**

The torrontés variety deserves to be much better known and appreciated, and maybe harnessing it to pinot grigio will help. The result here is a richly aromatic wine that shows lovely concentrated flavours that are defined and quite complex. It's zesty and fresh, and an excellent choice for spicy Asian-influenced dishes that feature pork, poultry or tofu.

NOTES

....

....

....

....

★ ★ ★ ★

FuZion Chenin/Chardonnay 2013

MENDOZA $7.95   (119800) **D**

When FuZion frenzy first hit Ontario, the object of mass adoration was the shiraz/malbec. Since then, the Zuccardi family, which owns the winery, has added more varieties, including this attractive white. It delivers very pleasant flavours that are full and fruity, and they come with a fresh, crisp texture that makes for easy drinking. Enjoy it on its own or with spicy chicken or seafood. It's a natural for Asian dishes.

NOTES

....

....

....

....

★ ★ ★ ★

Graffigna 'Centenario' Reserve Pinot Grigio 2013

SAN JUAN $12.95 (164756) **XD**

Yes, there are Argentine wines from regions other than Mendoza! This one, from an arid region just to the north of Mendoza, shows lovely fruit flavours and a vibrant and refreshing texture. It's dry and medium bodied, and it's the sort of wine you can enjoy on its own or with food. If you're bringing it to the table, bring along dishes featuring poultry or pork, or cream-based pasta.

NOTES

....

....

....

....

★ ★ ★ ★

Lurton Pinot Grigio 2013

VALLE DE UCO, MENDOZA $12.95 (556746) **XD**

Lurton is an unusual company in that it makes wine under the same name in many countries. This pinot grigio from its Argentine winery in Mendoza delivers quite delicious and intense aromas and flavours. It's plush, mouth filling and quite stylish, and has food-friendly edginess. It's a terrific choice for sipping on its own or drinking with spicy seafood and chicken or much Asian cuisine.

NOTES
....
....
....
....

NEW!
★ ★ ★ ★

UMA Collection Torrontés 2013

MENDOZA $10.30 (276626) **D**

Torrontés is Argentina's signature white grape variety, and here it makes an easy-drinking wine that you can enjoy on its own or with poultry, pork, white fish and seafood. The flavours are nicely concentrated and defined, and they're balanced by a broad seam of refreshing acidity.

NOTES
....
....
....
....

AUSTRALIA

AUSTRALIA GRABBED THE ATTENTION of international wine drinkers in the 1990s and, despite some ups and downs, it still has a good grip. Although better known for red wine, especially shiraz, it also produces a wide range of whites. The most common white variety in Australia is chardonnay, but others, such as the popular semillon/sauvignon blanc blend, also cross the Pacific Ocean.

The regional designation often found on Australian wine labels is South Eastern Australia, a huge zone that includes more than 90 percent of Australia's wine production and most of its designated wine regions. But Australian wineries are now stressing the importance of region, rather than just grape variety, in understanding their wines. In this list of Australian whites you'll find wines from well-known regions such as South Australia and the Barossa Valley, but also from lesser-known areas such as Eden Valley and Adelaide Hills.

Fifth Leg Semillon/Sauvignon Blanc 2012

★ ★ ★ ★ ½

WESTERN AUSTRALIA $15.95 (212613) **XD**

The semillon/sauvignon blanc combination is a classic from Bordeaux. Here, far away in Western Australia, it produces a lovely white that's substantial and crisp and that makes an excellent pairing with grilled white fish, seafood, shellfish and many curried dishes. The flavours are richly textured and the texture itself is both solid and vibrantly mouth-watering.

NOTES

....
....
....
....
....

NEW!

★ ★ ★ ★ ½

Fowles 'Are you Game?' Chardonnay 2012

VICTORIA $15.95 (359984) **D**

This is an elegant chardonnay that's tailored for game, according to the producers. A turkey on the label gives you the idea, but don't let that stop you from pairing it with chicken, pork or fish. It's a very attractive chardonnay, whose solid but not overbearing fruit shows complexity and structure. The acidity shines through, fresh and clean, and the whole is very well balanced.

NOTES

....
....
....
....
....

★ ★ ★ ★ ½

Grant Burge 'Summers' Chardonnay 2012

EDEN VALLEY/ADELAIDE HILLS $17.95 (269829) **XD**

This is a lovely chardonnay, with plenty of well-focused and complex flavours that are complemented by a broad seam of brisk, fresh acidity. All components work well here. It's a very versatile food wine that goes as well with roast chicken and pork as with grilled white fish and seafood.

NOTES

....
....
....
....

★ ★ ★ ★ ½

Jacob's Creek Reserve Chardonnay 2012

ADELAIDE HILLS $14.95 (270017) **XD**

Jacob's Creek is a small tributary that flows into the Chardonnay River—in a vinous sense, not geographically. Here you find a stylish chardonnay with layered, ripe flavours that are consistent right through the palate. The texture is round and smooth, with tanginess to keep your palate awake. Sip it on its own or drink it with roast or grilled chicken, turkey or pork, or with medium-strength cheeses.

NOTES

....

....

....

....

★ ★ ★ ★ ½

Jacob's Creek Reserve Riesling 2013

BAROSSA VALLEY $14.95 (212704) **XD**

Most of the grapes were grown in the higher altitudes of the Eden Valley, a sub-region of Barossa, where they picked up the juicy acidity you can feel when you sip this delicious wine. With focused fruit flavours and bright juiciness, it's a natural for fatty things like oysters and smoked salmon, but it also stretches to sushi and many Asian dishes.

NOTES

....

....

....

....

....

★ ★ ★ ★

Lindemans 'Bin 65' Chardonnay 2013

SOUTH EASTERN AUSTRALIA $10.95 (142117) **XD**

Bin 65 was designed specifically for the Canadian market because of the popularity of this style of wine here. Launched in 1985, it quickly became an icon throughout the world. Year after year, it delivers solid, ripe fruit flavours, a clean, smooth and slightly edgy texture, and good balance. It isn't too much of anything but has enough of everything to make it a versatile food wine. Drink it with roast pork or chicken.

NOTES

....

....

....

....

★ ★ ★ ★

Lindemans 'Bin 85' Pinot Grigio 2013

SOUTH EASTERN AUSTRALIA $10.95 (668947) **XD**

This is a straightforward, crisp and flavourful pinot grigio that goes well with roast chicken and pork and grilled white fish, as well as many summer salads. It's very dry and shows very good balance, with concentrated fruit flavours and a nice line of acidity that makes it vibrant and refreshing.

NOTES

....

....

....

....

....

★ ★ ★ ★ ½

McWilliam's 'Hanwood Estate' Chardonnay 2012

SOUTH EASTERN AUSTRALIA $13.95 (557934) **XD**

This medium-bodied, premium chardonnay gets marks for elegance in addition to its other positive qualities. It delivers lovely, rich, complex flavours with a subtle hint of oak, and everything is lifted by the remarkably refreshing and clean texture. It's fruity but dry, and it's an excellent choice when you're serving chicken, fish, pork or perhaps seafood in a cream sauce.

NOTES

....

....

....

....

NEW!
★ ★ ★ ★

McWilliam's 'Hanwood Estate' Moscato 2012

SOUTH EASTERN AUSTRALIA $13.95 (212696) **S**

Moscato is a popular variety for lovers of sweeter wines, because it is often made into styles like this one. It has a wide range of fruit flavours and a nice dose of sweetness, but it also has enough acidity to carry the sweetness off without its becoming cloying. Chill it down and drink it on its own, or pair it with sweeter (but not too sweet) fruit or berry desserts.

NOTES

....

....

....

....

....

Penfolds 'Koonunga Hill' Chardonnay 2012

★ ★ ★ ★ ½

SOUTH AUSTRALIA $14.95 (321943) **XD**

Dr. Christopher Penfold started making wine in Australia in the 1840s and prescribed it to his settler patients for the anemia many suffered after their long voyage from Britain. Now we drink it for pleasure, and you can certainly enjoy the intense, ripe fruit flavours in this chardonnay. It's medium bodied and very well balanced, and has a rich, attractive texture. Drink it with roast pork or turkey.

NOTES

....
....
....
....

Shingleback 'Haycutters' Sauvignon Blanc/Semillon 2012

★ ★ ★ ★

ADELAIDE HILLS/MCLAREN VALE $15.80 (207365) **XD**

This blend brings together the fruit and vibrancy of sauvignon blanc and the rounder texture of semillon. Originally from Bordeaux, the combination has been popularized in Australia with fine examples like this. Here you'll find solid fruit flavours with good concentration harnessed to bright acidity, and a crisp yet full texture. It's a great partner for rich fish, seafood, poultry and pork dishes.

NOTES

....
....
....
....

NEW!
Tic Tok Pocketwatch Chardonnay 2012
★ ★ ★ ★ ½

CENTRAL RANGES $14.95 (187104) **D**

From the Central Ranges wine region of New South Wales, this is a well-made chardonnay that combines weight and elegance. The fruit is concentrated and plush, but with good structure and complexity, and the well-calibrated acidity shines through fresh and clean. This is several cuts above most chardonnays, and it's very versatile. Drink it with white fish and seafood, or with poultry and pork.

NOTES

....
....
....
....

Wolf Blass 'Yellow Label' Chardonnay 2012

★ ★ ★ ★

SOUTH AUSTRALIA $14.95 (226860) XD

Wolf Blass 'Yellow Label' cabernet sauvignon was Wolfie's first big hit in Ontario, and now LCBO shelves have more of his mellow-yellow labels. The fruit is forward and this style of chardonnay has wide appeal. What give it quality and value are the complexity of the flavours and the refreshing acidity, which make this a great choice for fish, chicken or pork dishes.

NOTES

....

....

....

....

Wyndham Estate 'Bin 222' Chardonnay 2012

★ ★ ★ ★

SOUTH EASTERN AUSTRALIA $12.95   (93401) XD

So many chardonnays, and yet some stand out from the crowd. This is one. Your first impression will be the smoothness of the texture. It seems to glide effortlessly across your palate, filling your mouth with concentrated and nuanced flavours as it does so. For all that, it's more than just fruity, and it has all the refreshing acidity needed for chicken, salmon, turkey and pork.

NOTES

....

....

....

....

AUSTRIA

AUSTRIAN WINE IS BECOMING better known outside Europe, largely because of white wines made from the grüner veltliner grape variety. The other major white grape is riesling. The largest region is Niederösterreich (Lower Austria), which includes well-known appellations such as Kamptal, Kremstal and Wachau.

★ ★ ★ ★   **Grooner Grüner Veltliner 2012**

NIEDERÖSTERREICH $15.05 (168625) **XD**

Although the brand of this wine is a bit of a groaner, grüner veltliner has become Austria's signature white. It is generally—like this one—made in an easy-drinking style that pairs successfully with food. Here you'll find nicely concentrated, modestly complex flavours paired with crisp, fresh acidity. It's a very good choice for white fish, seafood, chicken and pork.

NOTES

....

....

....

....

BRITISH COLUMBIA

BRITISH COLUMBIA'S WINERIES produce many quality and value-priced white wines, but you won't find very many on LCBO shelves. Don't blame the LCBO. The reason is that British Columbians love their wine and drink most of what's made in their province. Much of the rest is sold in western Canada and in the US states to the south of British Columbia, rather than shipped all the way to Ontario.

The Vintners Quality Alliance (VQA) classification on British Columbia wine labels means that the grapes were grown in the region specified and that the wine has been tested and tasted by a panel.

Mission Hill Reserve Chardonnay 2012

★ ★ ★ ★ ½

VQA OKANAGAN VALLEY $19.95 (545004) **D**

[Vintages Essential] Mission Hill is the Okanagan Valley's iconic winery, a tourist destination that attracts crowds to see its architecture and its site, and to taste its well-made wines. This chardonnay is rich and elegant with intense, upfront fruit flavours and a smooth, mouth-filling texture. It's nicely balanced with the crispness needed to make it work well with food. Try it with grilled salmon or roast pork.

NOTES

....

....

....

....

CALIFORNIA

A WIDE RANGE OF WHITE GRAPES grow in California's vineyards, but the state is best known for chardonnay, its most popular and widely planted variety. Still, don't overlook other quality whites, especially pinot grigio and sauvignon blanc. Napa Valley is California's most famous region, but others, like Sonoma County and Central Coast, as well as smaller appellations like Paso Robles and Lodi, are becoming better known. Some of the California white wines in this book are designated simply "California," which means that producers can source grapes from any region throughout the state.

Beringer 'Founders' Estate' Chardonnay 2012

★ ★ ★ ★ ½

CALIFORNIA $16.95 (534230) **D**

The "founders" here are the Beringer boys, brothers Jacob and Frederick, who founded the winery in the 1870s. They'd be proud of this chardonnay, which delivers so well in every respect. The flavours are rich, well defined and complex, while the texture is plush, smooth, mouth filling and refreshing. The combination is a winner that you'll enjoy with richer chicken, pork and seafood dishes.

NOTES

....
....
....
....

Beringer 'Founders' Estate' Pinot Grigio 2012

★ ★ ★ ★ ½

CALIFORNIA $16.95 (45641) **XD**

This is a delicious pinot grigio that delivers real stylishness and elegance. The flavours are well defined with both concentration and delicacy, and the texture shows a beautiful balance of acidity and fruit. It's silky smooth and has a refreshing quality that suits food, although you could savour it on its own, too. If you're thinking of pairing this with a meal, try a delicately spiced Thai dish.

NOTES

....
....
....
....

Bonterra Chardonnay 2012

★ ★ ★ ★ ★

MENDOCINO COUNTY $18.95 (342436) **D**

[Vintages Essential] Bonterra grows its grapes organically—that is, without the use of chemical fertilizers, pesticides or any other treatment. Whether or not it shows in your experience of the wine is debatable, but there's no debate that this is a fine chardonnay. It combines power (intense fruit flavours) with finesse (a refined and balanced texture) and is a great choice for chicken, pork and white fish.

NOTES

....
....
....
....

Chateau St. Jean Chardonnay 2012

★ ★ ★ ★ ★

SONOMA COUNTY $18.95 (269738) **XD**

This is an attractive and elegant chardonnay that shows ripe, vibrant fruit and fresh, clean acidity. The flavours are complex, full and slightly plush, with the oak enhancing the texture more than interfering with the fruit purity. With terrific balance, this goes beautifully with richer chicken, pork and seafood dishes.

NOTES

....

....

....

....

....

Fetzer 'Shaly Loam' Gewürztraminer 2012

★ ★ ★ ★

CALIFORNIA $11.95 (222778) **M**

All Fetzer wines come from vineyards that are farmed sustainably with attention to the environment and energy use. This off-dry gewürztraminer is made in a rich, plush, fruit-forward style, with layers and layers of sweet fruit from start to finish. It's kept honest and fresh with a nice line of acidity, and it's a great choice for spicy Asian dishes.

NOTES

....

....

....

....

....

Fetzer 'Valley Oaks' Pinot Grigio 2012

★ ★ ★ ★

CALIFORNIA $11.95 (34041) **XD**

This is about as dry as you can get (0.2 grams of residual sugar), but it has pretty aromatics and is full of attractive, fruity flavours, partly thanks to the addition of a little viognier and moscato. It's light to medium in weight and very well balanced, with clean, crisp acidity. It's also versatile: enjoy it on its own or with seafood, fish, poultry or salads.

NOTES

....

....

....

....

....

Hess 'Select' Chardonnay 2011

★ ★ ★ ★

MONTEREY COUNTY　　　　　　　　$15.95 (270074) **XD**

California chardonnays have a reputation, deserved or not, for being over-oaked. Try this one as an example of smartly used oak. It's just perceptible in the aromas and a little less so in the flavours, but it adds a little *je ne sais quoi* to an already good complexity. With fresh, clean acidity and a smooth texture, this is a good choice for many seafood and white fish dishes as well as for pork and chicken.

NOTES

....

....

....

....

J. Lohr 'Riverstone' Chardonnay 2012

★ ★ ★ ★ ★

ARROYO SECO, MONTEREY　　　　$18.95　(258699)　**D**

[Vintages Essential] This is a stylish and opulent chardonnay from the little-known Arroyo Seco wine region in central California. Here you get plush, ripe and multi-faceted fruit flavours that sit harmoniously with a texture that's full, round and refreshing. It's dry and medium bodied and very well balanced. Enjoy this with herbed roast chicken, grilled salmon, pork tenderloin or seared scallops or lobster.

NOTES

....

....

....

....

Ménage à Trois White 2011

★ ★ ★ ★

CALIFORNIA　　　　　　　　　　$16.95　(308015)　**D**

Made (of course) from three grape varieties—chardonnay, moscato and chenin blanc—this is a wine you can enjoy on its own or with food. For the latter, good pairings would be chicken, turkey or pork, or some lightly spicy Asian dishes that feature these meats. Look for aromatic flavours that are consistent right through, as well as good acid–fruit balance that gives the wine a refreshing character.

NOTES

....

....

....

....

Montevina Pinot Grigio 2012

★ ★ ★ ★

CALIFORNIA $14.95 (237750) D

There's lots of sweet, ripe fruit in this pinot grigio. It doesn't offer too much complexity, but it's attractive in flavour and the fruit is balanced by clean, crisp acidity. This dry, medium-weight white goes well with many styles of food. Try it with roast chicken or pork, white fish, seafood or not-too-spicy dishes.

NOTES

Raymond 'Family Classic' Chardonnay 2010

★ ★ ★ ★ ½

NORTH COAST $15.95 (269753) XD

You've got to love this style of chardonnay. It speaks Californian, with plush, full-on fruit that holds solid from start to finish. The oak is well managed and enhances the texture without interfering with the fruit purity, and the acidity lifts the fruit and makes the whole thing fresh. This is a chardonnay that goes well with richer seafood, fish, poultry and pork dishes.

NOTES

Robert Mondavi Chardonnay 2011

★ ★ ★ ★ ½

NAPA VALLEY $26.00 (310409) XD

This is an elegant chardonnay that combines plush and intensely flavoured fruit with clean, fresh acidity. The tension makes for a juicy, mouth-filling flavour and the weighty but refreshing texture suits it for richer varieties of seafood (lobster, scallops) or cream-based seafood, fish or white meat dishes.

NOTES

NEW!
★ ★ ★ ★ ½

Robert Mondavi Fumé Blanc 2011

CALIFORNIA $22.75 (221887) XD

[Vintages Essential] Fumé blanc is Mondavi's name for a style of sauvignon blanc. Wanting to elevate sauvignon blanc's image, he made a drier, more complex style that reminded him of Pouilly-Fumé, the French region known for sauvignon. This wine lives up to his aspirations, showing complexity, concentration and some elegance. Enjoy it with white fish, seafood and pork dishes.

NOTES
....
....
....
....

★ ★ ★ ★ ½

Robert Mondavi 'Private Selection' Chardonnay 2012

CENTRAL COAST $16.95 (379180) D

Try this on any chardonnay-skeptic—you know, the people who loudly declare that they don't like chardonnay, as if that's something to be proud of. Chardonnay comes in so many styles, and this is a particularly attractive one. It's medium to full bodied and has a smooth texture and lovely concentrated flavours. It's a versatile, fruit-filled chardonnay that goes as well with roast chicken as with grilled salmon.

NOTES
....
....
....
....

★ ★ ★ ★

Robert Mondavi 'Private Selection' Sauvignon Blanc 2012

CENTRAL COAST $16.95 (405753) XD

This is a very good sauvignon blanc for food, and I'd be happy to drink it with white fish, seafood with a spritz of lemon, or lemon chicken, for that matter. It doesn't have the flavour power of some sauvignon blancs (like many from New Zealand), but it's very solid, attractive and well balanced and has the refreshing and clean texture you want in this variety.

NOTES
....
....
....
....

★ ★ ★ ★

Santa Barbara Collection Chardonnay 2010

SANTA BARBARA COUNTY · $18.95 (308114) **XD**

This is made in a fairly lean style, with the fruit well focused and defined and carrying a pretty veneer of oak. The acidity comes through clear and clean, giving some juiciness to the texture. Overall, it's very well balanced and attractive and a good partner for poultry, white fish and seafood, as well as milder cheeses.

NOTES

....

....

....

....

....

NEW!
★ ★ ★ ★

Sterling 'Vintner's Collection' Chardonnay 2012

CENTRAL COAST · $15.95 (669242) **D**

This is a fairly classic west coast style of chardonnay, with hints of oak in its aromas and flavours. Far from being overbearing, the oak is well managed and lets the rich fruit of the flavours shine through. The acidity is well balanced, and all the components are well integrated. This is a very good choice for many richer poultry and pork dishes.

NOTES

....

....

....

....

★ ★ ★ ★ ½

Toasted Head Chardonnay 2012

CALIFORNIA · $17.95 (594341) **D**

[Vintages Essential] 'Toasted Head' refers to the practice of charring the insides of barrels. Often the ends (heads) are not toasted, but in the barrels used to age this chardonnay, they were. This is a bold and assertive chardonnay with intense flavours and a round texture, but it carries the liveliness needed to pair well with food. Drink it with grilled salmon, pork tenderloin or herbed roast chicken.

NOTES

....

....

....

Wente 'Morning Fog' Chardonnay 2012

★ ★ ★ ★ ½

LIVERMORE VALLEY/SAN FRANCISCO BAY $16.95 (175430)   D

The morning fog is important to many California wine regions. It swirls up the river valleys at dawn and keeps the vines cool until it eventually dissipates in late morning or early afternoon. The results are chardonnays like this that retain wonderful freshness of flavour and texture while having concentrated fruit and a round, silky mouthfeel. It's a delicious wine with chicken, turkey or pork.

NOTES

....

....

....

....

Woodbridge Moscato 2012

★ ★ ★ ★

CALIFORNIA $11.95   (199216)   M

Among the moscatos currently in the LCBO, this is one of the sweetest. It has all the hallmarks of the popular style—sweetness, aromatics, fruitiness and decent acidity—but the sweetness here stands out. If you like sipping sweet wines, this is for you, but many more people will find it a good pairing with rich foods like foie gras and spicy Asian dishes.

NOTES

....

....

....

....

Woodbridge Sauvignon Blanc 2012

★ ★ ★ ★

CALIFORNIA $11.95   (40501)   XD

There's a world of sauvignon blanc out there, from the big and pungent style popularized by New Zealand to the understated style more common in northern France. This inexpensive California example is vibrant and zesty, with nicely defined flavours that are bright and fresh. No question that this is destined for shellfish, seafood or fish that's been subjected to a squeeze of fresh lemon.

NOTES

....

....

....

....

CHILE

ALTHOUGH CHILE IS BETTER KNOWN for its red wines, many of its whites deliver great quality and value. The warm growing conditions in most of Chile's wine regions have led many producers to seek out cooler areas (like the Casablanca Valley) and to plant white grape vines at higher (and cooler) altitudes. The main white varieties planted are chardonnay and sauvignon blanc, but there are others.

Designated Chilean wine regions are indicated after the letters "DO" (*Denominación de Origen*).

Caliterra Reserva Sauvignon Blanc 2013

★ ★ ★ ★ ½

DO CASABLANCA VALLEY $9.95   (275909) **XD**

The regions generally considered best for sauvignon blanc are the Loire Valley in France and Marlborough in New Zealand, but Chile produces well-priced competition. This one, made from grapes grown in one of Chile's prime sauvignon blanc regions, has a crisp, refreshing texture and vibrant, fresh fruit flavours. It's medium bodied and goes well with a goat cheese salad or with fish or seafood juiced with fresh lemon.

NOTES

....
....
....
....

Casillero del Diablo Reserva Sauvignon Blanc 2013

★ ★ ★ ★

DO CASABLANCA/LIMARI/RAPEL VALLEYS $11.95 (578641) **XD**

This has everything you want from a well-made sauvignon blanc. It shows flavours that are concentrated and complex and a texture that's both tangy and refreshing. Dry and medium bodied, it goes very well with white fish and seafood (and fish and chips) with a squeeze of lemon, or a tomato and goat cheese tart.

NOTES

....
....
....
....

Cono Sur 'Bicicleta' Viognier 2013

★ ★ ★ ★ ★

DO COLCHAGUA VALLEY $9.95   (64287) **XD**

You can make this your go-to white when you're eating spicy Thai or Indian dishes. It has rich, delicious, sweet fruit flavours and a refreshing texture, all of which tend to tame the spiciness a little without interfering with the flavours. Viognier is an underappreciated variety, and this one comes from a winery that has pioneered many sustainable practices in its vineyards.

NOTES

....
....
....
....
....

Cono Sur Reserva Chardonnay 2012

★ ★ ★ ★

DO CASABLANCA VALLEY $12.95 (270066) **XD**

The vineyards are in the cool Casablanca Valley, where the sun ripens the grapes and the cool breeze from the Pacific allows the acidity to develop. The result is a lovely, refreshing, well-balanced wine with sweet fruit flavours and very good complexity. Enjoy this with poultry, white fish, seafood and pork.

NOTES

....

....

....

....

....

Errazuriz 'Estate' Chardonnay 2013

★ ★ ★ ★

DO CASABLANCA VALLEY $12.95 (318741) **XD**

Chile's Casablanca Valley appellation is an area where the vines are cooled by breezes from the nearby Pacific Ocean. The coolness promotes the development of acidity and the sunshine ripens the grapes, and one result is this chardonnay. Here you find sweet, ripe fruit—well focused and concentrated—and fresh acidity working harmoniously together. It's great with poultry, pork and white fish.

NOTES

....

....

....

....

Errazuriz 'Max Reserva' Sauvignon Blanc 2013

★ ★ ★ ★

DO ACONCAGUA COSTA $15.95 (273342) **XD**

This sauvignon shows very good weight and a fairly dense texture. The fruit is solid, layered and consistent from start to finish, and the acidity shows through well, making this a refreshing, if substantial, white. Drink it with the usual sauvignon suspects, like white fish and seafood, but also try it with medium-heat curries.

NOTES

....

....

....

....

★ ★ ★ ★

Santa Carolina 'Leyda Estate' Reserva Sauvignon Blanc 2013

DO LEYDA VALLEY $11.95 (337535) **XD**

Made from grapes grown in one of Chile's cool wine regions, close to the Pacific coast and its cold winds, this sauvignon is crisp and refreshing. The fruit is bright and vibrant with good complexity, and the fruit–acid balance sets it up for food. This is a great choice for seafood and white fish, and for fish and chips (with lemon, not vinegar).

NOTES

....

....

....

....

★ ★ ★ ★ ½

Santa Rita '120' Sauvignon Blanc 2013

DO CENTRAL VALLEY $9.95 (23606) **XD**

Sauvignon blanc has been "discovered" in the last ten years and this has led to plantings in many different conditions. In turn, several different styles have emerged, and this example from Santa Rita sits in the middle ground. Dry and very well balanced, it delivers full flavours and retains the tangy zestiness that makes sauvignon blanc such a great wine when you're having white fish and seafood.

NOTES

....

....

....

....

★ ★ ★ ★ ½

Santa Rita Reserva Chardonnay 2012

DO CASABLANCA VALLEY $13.95 (348359) **XD**

Santa Rita is one of Chile's established wineries, but it doesn't rest on its well-deserved laurels. This Casablanca chardonnay is grown in a relatively recently developed cool region that produces fresh, crisp, well-focused wines. The flavours are concentrated, the texture tangy and refreshing and the overall image very attractive. Serve it with pork tenderloin or roast chicken.

NOTES

....

....

....

....

Santa Rita Reserva Sauvignon Blanc 2013

★ ★ ★ ★

DO CASABLANCA VALLEY $13.95 (275677) **XD**

Sauvignon blanc is popular because of its characteristic crispness and clean, pungent notes, which it develops when the grapes grow in cooler areas. The vineyards in Chile's Casablanca Valley are fanned by cold breezes that blow in from the Pacific Ocean early each afternoon. They give zesty texture and lovely flavours to this sauvignon blanc, which is a great choice for fish or seafood with a squeeze of lemon.

NOTES

....

....

....

....

FRANCE

THE NUMEROUS FRENCH WINE REGIONS produce whites from many different varieties of grapes. Some regions are closely tied to specific grapes, like Burgundy to chardonnay and Sancerre to sauvignon blanc, but others are not. You'll find a wide range of varieties and styles in this list.

French wine labels display a few terms worth knowing. Wines labelled *Appellation d'Origine Contrôlée* (abbreviated AOC in this book) or *Appellation d'Origine Protégée* (AOP) are wines in the highest-quality classification in France. They're made under tight rules that regulate such aspects as the grape varieties that can be used in each region.

Wines labelled *Vin de Pays* or IGP (*Indication Géographique Protégée*) are regional wines made with fewer restrictions. They must be good quality, but producers have much more flexibility in the grapes they can use and how much wine they can make. *Vins de Pays d'Oc* (the ancient region of Occitanie) are by far the most important of the *Vins de Pays* wines.

★ ★ ★ ★

Baron de Hoen Réserve Pinot Gris 2012

AOC ALSACE $16.35 (280149) **D**

This is a luscious, off-dry pinot gris that's an excellent bet for many spicy dishes featuring pork, poultry, seafood or vegetables. The flavours are rich, almost pungent, and the texture carries a hint of viscosity. But both fruit and texture are reined in by a terrific seam of acidity, giving the wine balance and the freshness needed for food.

NOTES

....

....

....

....

★ ★ ★ ★

Bouchard Père & Fils Mâcon-Lugny Saint-Pierre 2012

AOC MÂCON-LUGNY $15.95 (51573) **XD**

This is from a designated area in the Mâcon region in southern Burgundy. Made from 100 percent chardonnay, it's an elegant wine that delivers nicely concentrated flavours that are soft and stylish. The texture is quite rich and creamy, with a seam of acidity that makes it very refreshing. This is an excellent wine for grilled salmon and for meats like chicken, turkey and pork.

NOTES

....

....

....

....

★ ★ ★ ★ ½

Bouchard Père & Fils Petit Chablis 2012

AOC PETIT CHABLIS $19.95 (51466) **XD**

Petit Chablis is one of the appellations (designated regions) of Burgundy's broader Chablis region, and it's often dismissed, partly because of the low minimum alcohol (this one is 12 percent). But this is ideal if you want a lower-alcohol wine, especially during summer's heat. The flavours are restrained, focused and well-defined. It's very refreshing and a very good match for chicken, white fish and seafood.

NOTES

....

....

....

....

....

Bouchard Père & Fils Pouilly-Fuissé 2012

★ ★ ★ ★ ★

AOC POUILLY-FUISSÉ $27.90   (56580) **XD**

Pouilly-Fuissé is a prestigious region in southern Burgundy that produces only white wine and grows only chardonnay. Don't expect to see this labelled as a chardonnay, though, as the regional name has all the cachet. This one is gorgeous and stylish, with pure, nuanced flavours and a beautifully smooth and clean texture. Medium weight and dry, it's a great choice for poultry, pork, fish or seafood.

NOTES

....

....

....

....

Brumont Gros Manseng Sauvignon 2012

★ ★ ★ ★

IGP CÔTES DE GASCOGNE $12.95 (297234) **XD**

This blend of gros manseng—a variety native to southwest France—and sauvignon blanc is very versatile. It's great drinking on its own, as an aperitif or with spicy fish, poultry or pork dishes. It delivers crisp acidity and vibrant fruity flavours, both in good balance, and it's dry and mid-weight.

NOTES

....

....

....

....

....

NEW!
★ ★ ★ ★

Domaine de Pellehaut 'Harmonie de Gascogne' Blanc 2012

IGP CÔTES DE GASCOGNE $13.35 (319665) **XD**

Made from four varieties (ugni blanc, colombard, sauvignon, and chardonnay) in the southwest of France, this is a refreshing and flavourful white that you can enjoy on its own or with white fish and poultry. The flavours are quite generous, the texture is round and smooth, and the acidity shines through crisply and cleanly.

NOTES

....

....

....

....

Domaine Laroche 'Saint Martin' Chablis 2012

★ ★ ★ ★ ½

AOC CHABLIS $22.95   (289124)   **D**

Domaine Laroche is one of the most prestigious producers of chablis. Made from chardonnay, this delivers quality from start to finish. Look for lovely, elegant flavours that are focused and subtly layered, and a texture that's rich, refined and fresh. This is an excellent choice for shellfish, seafood, white fish and poultry.

NOTES

....

....

....

....

....

Dopff & Irion Gewürztraminer 2012

★ ★ ★ ★

AOC ALSACE $15.45   (81463)   **D**

Gewürztraminer is one of the key grapes of Alsace, in eastern France, which has become known as a region whose wines go well with Asian food. This pungent, spicy, just off-dry wine has good intensity and the right amount of acidity to complement and rein in the flavours without interfering with their enjoyment. Try it yourself with Asian cuisine.

NOTES

....

....

....

....

....

NEW!

★ ★ ★ ★ ½

Guy Saget Sancerre 2012

AOC SANCERRE $21.95 (319657) **XD**

Sancerre, located at the eastern end of the long Loire Valley wine region, is noted for its sauvignon blanc wines that are generally known by the name of the region, not for the variety. This one offers the classic Sancerre qualities of restrained but concentrated flavours, good complexity and a vibrant platform of fresh acidity. It's dry and harmonious, and is a great partner for many poultry and white fish dishes.

NOTES

....

....

....

....

★ ★ ★ ★ ½

Henri Bourgeois 'Les Baronnes' Sancerre 2012

AOC SANCERRE $24.95 (542548) XD

[Vintages Essential] Sancerre is a notable appellation for sauvignon blanc, and Henri Bourgeois is one of the main producers. (He also established a winery in New Zealand's Marlborough, another region known for sauvignon.) This wine delivers concentrated but restrained flavours, with impressive structure and complexity. The acidity shines through, and it's a great choice for many white fish and seafood dishes, as well as for chicken.

NOTES

....
....
....
....

★ ★ ★ ★

Jaffelin Bourgogne Aligoté 2012

AOC BOURGOGNE ALIGOTÉ $16.45   (53868) XD

Aligoté is a Burgundian grape variety that's perhaps best known for the wine used with cassis in making the aperitif kir. But it also makes worthy wine in its own right, as this example shows. It delivers attractive, fairly understated flavours, with a quite taut but balanced texture from the acidity. It makes a very good accompaniment to grilled white fish, trout and roast chicken.

NOTES

....
....
....
....

★ ★ ★ ★ ½

Joseph Drouhin 'Drouhin-Vaudon' Chablis 2012

AOC CHABLIS $21.95 (284026) XD

There are lovely ripe aromas on the nose here. When you get the wine into your mouth they are more understated, but they're solid and consistent right through to the finish and show plenty of complexity. The acidity is bright and fresh, lifting the fruit and setting you up for food. This is an excellent choice for grilled white fish, herbed roast chicken and mild cheeses.

NOTES

....
....
....

★ ★ ★ ★ ½

Joseph Drouhin Pouilly-Fuissé 2012

AOC POUILLY-FUISSE $26.70 (361683) **XD**

Only white wine (from chardonnay) is made in Pouilly-Fuissé, which is one of Burgundy's most highly rated white wine appellations. This is quite an elegant example, in which all the components are well integrated. The fruit is pure and focused, and it's finely balanced by the supporting, clean, fresh acidity. Think of this when you're serving roasted or grilled poultry, pork or white fish.

NOTES

....

....

....

....

NEW!
★ ★ ★ ★ ½

L'Arjolle Sauvignon Blanc-Viognier 2012

IGP CÔTES DE THONGUE $12.35 (348904) **D**

This lovely, fresh blend of sauvignon and viognier shows quality and value across the board. The fruit is well structured and layered, and it's consistent from attack to finish. The supporting acidity is vibrant and clean, and it delivers an almost juicy texture. All the components are well integrated. It's an excellent choice for white fish and seafood dishes, but don't by any means rule it out if you're serving poultry or pork.

NOTES

....

....

....

....

★ ★ ★ ★ ★

La Chablisienne 'Les Vénérables' Vieilles Vignes Chablis 2010

AOC CHABLIS $24.95 (215525) **XD**

[Vintages Essential] There's no standard definition of "old vines" (*vieilles vignes*), but producers often use the term because older vines produce small quantities of higher-quality grapes. This is certainly a delicious and elegant chablis (made from chardonnay), with stylish and nuanced flavours and a smooth, refreshing texture. Everything is in fine harmony and balance. Serve this with simply prepared fish, chicken or pork dishes.

NOTES

....

....

....

La Croix d'Azur Sauvignon Blanc 2011

IGP CÔTES DE GASCOGNE $11.85 (330928) **XD**

This is a very attractive, well-measured sauvignon blanc that's as far from the assertive Marlborough style as . . . well, Marlborough is from southwest France. Look for well-focused fruit flavours here, somewhat understated but concentrated, nonetheless. The acidity is bright and fresh. This is a very good choice for many white fish, seafood and poultry dishes.

NOTES
....
....
....
....

Louis Bernard Côtes du Rhône White 2012

AOC CÔTES DU RHÔNE $13.10 (589432) **XD**

Made from grenache blanc, bourboulenc and viognier, this dry, medium-bodied white blend delivers good quality across the board. The ripe flavours are consistent from start to finish, and they're very ably supported by a seam of acidity that makes the wine a palate-refreshing partner for food. Drink it with roast poultry or pork, or with grilled white fish or seafood.

NOTES
....
....
....
....

Louis Jadot Mâcon Villages Chardonnay 2012

AOC MÂCON VILLAGES $17.65 (164145) **XD**

Mâcon (pronounced mah-kon) is one of the many regions of Burgundy, and it is known for its white chardonnay-based wines. This one offers excellent fruit–acid balance, with nicely pitched and solid fruit on one side and refreshing, bright acidity on the other. It's medium bodied and dry and makes a great partner for grilled white fish, poultry or pork as well as for many cream-based fish and meat dishes.

NOTES
....
....
....
....

Louis Latour 'Ardèche' Chardonnay 2012

IGP ARDÈCHE $15.05 (132498) XD

This is a well-made and versatile dry chardonnay that goes well with pork, poultry, mild cheeses and many summer salads, as well as being good drinking on its own. Look for attractive flavours that are nicely concentrated, and good fruit–acid balance that makes for a refreshing texture.

NOTES

....
....
....
....

★ ★ ★ ★

Louis Latour Chardonnay 2011

AOC BOURGOGNE $17.95   (55533) XD

Nearly all white wines from Burgundy are made from chardonnay (as the reds are made from pinot noir). They vary in style from lean and acidic to plump and fruity. This is a mid-range style, with concentrated and nuanced flavours, a round and smooth (but refreshing) texture and very good balance. Drink it with chicken, turkey and soft mild cheeses like brie and camembert.

NOTES

....
....
....
....

★ ★ ★ ★ ½

M. Chapoutier 'Belleruche' Côtes du Rhône 2012

AOC CÔTES DU RHÔNE $15.95 (245340) XD

White côtes du Rhônes are not as common as their red siblings, but they are generally well worth looking for. This one (a blend of the grenache blanc, clairette, and bourboulenc varieties) shows very concentrated flavours, with good complexity and structure balanced very well with fresh, clean acidity. It's a great choice for meals of chicken, turkey, pork or white fish.

NOTES

....
....
....
....

Mouton Cadet Réserve Graves 2011

★ ★ ★ ★ ½

AOC GRAVES $15.25 (247080) **XD**

Graves is a small appellation in Bordeaux that is well known for its white wines. This blend of semillon, sauvignon blanc and muscadelle is attractive and stylish. The fruit is textured and nicely structured, with good complexity, and the acidity is clean and refreshing. It's dry and medium bodied and makes an excellent wine for seafood, shellfish and white fish dishes.

NOTES
....
....
....

Pierre Sparr Gewürztraminer 2012

★ ★ ★ ★

AOC ALSACE $16.05 (373373) **M**

Pierre Sparr is an Alsatian producer who does very well across his portfolio. This is a lovely, medium-bodied gewürztraminer with an opulent and plump texture that fills your mouth with flavour. As for those flavours, they're spicy, pungent and rich, with complexity to spare. If you're looking for a sparring partner for this wine, try a spicy Asian (especially Thai) dish.

NOTES
....
....
....
....

NEW!
★ ★ ★ ★ ½
Remoissenet Père et Fils 'Renommée' Bourgogne 2010

AOC BOURGOGNE $21.45 (337501) **XD**

This is a remarkably refreshing chardonnay that kicks off with a burst of acidity, paired with well-structured and layered fruit. The flavours hold true right through the palate, and they're ripe and sweet-centred, with just a subtle hint of oak. The balance is well done. This is a very good choice for richer poultry and pork dishes, perhaps those prepared in a cream-based sauce.

NOTES
....
....
....
....
....

★ ★ ★ ★

Remy Pannier Sauvignon Blanc 2012

AOC TOURAINE $13.95   (68676) **D**

From Touraine, in the long Loire Valley region, this sauvignon blanc delivers successfully across the board. The flavours are solid from start to finish and it's crisp and refreshing. This is a good bet for a wide range of foods, from seafood to chicken, from white fish to not-too-hot curries.

NOTES

....

....

....

....

....

★ ★ ★ ★

Sauvion 'Carte d'Or' Muscadet 2011

AOC MUSCADET SÈVRE-ET-MAINE $12.95 (143016) **XD**

Muscadet, from a Loire Valley region near the Atlantic coast, is France's most popular wine to serve with fish. It can be bland and light, but this one has well-defined fruit flavours. It's medium bodied with an appealing and tangy texture, and it goes very well with all kinds of seafood. Try it with grilled white fish or with mussels steamed in white wine.

NOTES

....

....

....

....

....

★ ★ ★ ★ ½

William Fèvre 'Champs Royaux' Chablis 2012

AOC CHABLIS $22.05 (276436) **XD**

The classic wines from Chablis are chardonnays made and aged in stainless steel tanks rather than in oak barrels. They offer pure, well-defined and complex fruit flavours like this one does. It has a refreshing texture—not plush and mouth filling, but very crisp and clean. It's medium bodied and an excellent match for seafood and shellfish. Try it with mussels steamed in white wine and herbs.

NOTES

....

....

....

....

....

Willm Réserve Gewürztraminer 2012

★ ★ ★ ★

AOC ALSACE $15.95 (269852) **M**

This is a classic style of gewürztraminer from Alsace. Look for plush, luscious fruit flavours that are quite intense and lingering, along with a good burst of acidity that makes another glass more than drinkable. This is an excellent choice for spicy dishes, and it's almost a classic match for Asian cuisine.

NOTES

....
....
....
....

Willy Gisselbrecht Riesling 2011

NEW!
★ ★ ★ ★

AOC ALSACE $14.45 (315309) **XD**

This is a very dry—you might say, astringent—riesling, with a burst of bracing acidity as one of its assets. But the fruit is clearly present: concentrated, ripe and complex in an understated way. The balance is very good for this style of riesling, and it's versatile at the table. Drink it with richer poultry and pork dishes, as well as with seafood and smoked salmon.

NOTES

....
....
....
....
....

Yvon Mau Colombard-Chardonnay 2012

NEW!
★ ★ ★ ★

IGP CÔTES DE GASCOGNE $8.95   (627265) **D**

Made from 75 percent colombard and 25 percent chardonnay, this is a straightforward and refreshing white that you can drink on its own or pair with a white fish, pork or poultry dish. You'll find solid and substantial flavours from start to finish, and good fruit-acid balance, with the acidity kicking in to freshen everything up.

NOTES

....
....
....
....
....

GERMANY

WONDERFUL, GOOD-VALUE GERMAN WHITE WINES appear often in the LCBO's Vintages section, but the selection on the LCBO General Purchase List is often disappointing. Many people are put off by German wines because they believe they're all sickly sweet. But most German wines are dry. While it's true that many quality German wines do have some sweetness, it's not fake and cloying. It comes from the richness of natural sugars in the grapes.

Important terms on German wine labels are *Prädikatswein* (the highest-quality classification of wine) and *Qualitätswein* (sometimes followed by *b.A.*, designating wines of quality but not of the highest level). Each of these terms is followed by the name of the wine region where the grapes were grown.

Carl Reh Riesling Kabinett 2012

★ ★ ★ ★ ½

PRÄDIKATSWEIN MOSEL $11.95 (174854) **M**

This is a delicious off-dry riesling that we can only hope is part of the renewal of German wine offerings in the LCBO. It delivers plenty of ripe, defined flavours supported by a seam of bright, lively acidity. It's refreshing and you could easily sip this on its own, or you could pair it with well-seasoned or spicy poultry, pork and seafood dishes.

NOTES

....

....

....

....

GREECE

GREECE DOESN'T FEATURE PROMINENTLY on many people's wine radar (until they visit the country), but it produces many good-value wines. Although international grape varieties are becoming more popular there, it's good to see that many wines are still made using indigenous varieties.

★ ★ ★ ★
Boutari Moschofilero 2012

PGI MANTINIA $11.95 (172387) **XD**

Moschofilero is a grape variety indigenous to Greece that produces aromatic wines with good acidity. This is true to type, and it's an excellent choice for roast chicken and pork and for spicy (think Asian) dishes of many kinds. The flavours are rich in spicy fruitiness and hold on right through the palate, and the acidity comes though clean and refreshing. It's definitely worth trying.

NOTES

....

....

....

....

★ ★ ★ ★
Hatzimichalis Chardonnay 2012

REGIONAL WINE OF ATALANTI VALLEY $14.95 (269654) **XD**

Although most Greek wines are made from indigenous grape varieties, some—like this chardonnay—are made from international varieties. This is well made and attractive, with vibrant and nicely concentrated fruit flavours balanced by clean acidity. It goes well with grilled fish and chicken (served with lemon, as they would in Greece) and with mild, creamy cheeses.

NOTES

....

....

....

....

HUNGARY

HUNGARIAN WINES MAKE LITTLE impact on the Canadian market, but they are starting to come into their own and are becoming more and more widely available. One of Hungary's best white grape varieties is hárslevelü, which can be used to make the country's iconic sweet wine, tokaji.

Hungarovin Debrői Hárslevelü 2012

★ ★ ★ ★

AOP VDDETTE EREDETD KLASSZIKUS BOR $8.45 (536268)   **M**

Made from Hungary's signature white grape variety, hárslevelü, this is fairly sweet and fruity and shows a nice clean and crisp acidity that balances the sweetness effectively. It's a lighter white that makes a good choice with spicy seafood, chicken and white fish, as well as many lighter Asian dishes.

NOTES

....

....

....

....

ITALY

ITALY HAS A LONG HISTORY of producing white wines from indigenous grapes, but in recent years we've seen more from international varieties such as chardonnay. One international grape grown in many Italian regions is pinot grigio (also known as pinot gris). There are many mediocre pinot grigios, but this list identifies a number that stand out from the herd for quality and value.

The highest-quality classification of Italian wines is DOCG (*Denominazione di Origine Controllata e Garantita*), which indicates a wine made to stringent regulations and from a few specified grape varieties. Wines in the next category, DOC (*Denominazione di Origine Controllata*), follow similar rules. Wines labelled IGT (*Indicazione Geografica Tipica*) or IGP (*Indicazione Geografica Protetta*) are made according to even less stringent regulations and may use a wider range of grape varieties. This doesn't mean that a DOCG wine is necessarily better than an IGT/IGP. In fact, some of Italy's most famous wines are IGT/IGP wines. Overall, you'll find quality and value in all these categories, as this list shows.

Anselmi San Vincenzo 2013

★ ★ ★ ★

IGT VENETO $16.95   (948158) **D**

[Vintages Essential] From northeastern Italy, this is a blend of an Italian grape, garganega, and two international varieties, chardonnay and sauvignon blanc. It's a ménage à trois that really works. Look for sweet fruit in this dry wine, finely balanced by bright, crisp acidity. It's a great wine for summer sipping or as an aperitif, and it goes well with many seafood, fish and poultry dishes.

NOTES

....

....

....

....

Casal Thaulero Pinot Grigio 2013

★ ★ ★ ★

IGT TERRE SICILIANE $8.45   (73163) **D**

A few years ago it seemed that pinot grigio/pinot gris was going to outsell chardonnay, but chardonnay held on. This is a not-so-complex, dry, medium-bodied pinot grigio that goes well with slightly spicy dishes featuring seafood, chicken or pork. The flavours are sweet and fruity and they're nicely complemented by acidity that translates into a refreshing and tangy texture.

NOTES

....

....

....

....

Cavallina Grillo/Pinot Grigio 2012

★ ★ ★ ★ ½

IGT SICILIA $8.20   (123166) **D**

Grillo is a grape variety widely planted in Sicily, where it can withstand high temperatures. It produces high acidity that translates as a zesty, vibrant texture, the sort you see here. Blended with pinot grigio for fruit flavour, it makes an easy-drinking white on its own, or pairs well with spicy dishes and many ways of preparing chicken, white fish, shellfish and seafood.

NOTES

....

....

....

....

Citra Trebbiano d'Abruzzo 2012

★ ★ ★ ★

DOC TREBBIANO D'ABRUZZO $7.45   (522144) XD

Like many Italian wine names, this one combines a grape variety (trebbiano) and a region (Abruzzo). It's medium bodied and has an attractively dry feel. Look for very pleasant and fairly complex fruit flavours and a clean and refreshing texture that makes for a good match with creamy Italian dishes. Try it with fettuccine alfredo or any pasta prepared in a cream sauce.

NOTES

Danzante Pinot Grigio 2012

★ ★ ★ ★ ½

IGT DELLE VENEZIE $14.95   (26906) XD

"Dance the pure emotion of Italian wine," the label urges. Well, the texture in this pinot grigio is lively and refreshing, and it's in step with the flavours, which are nicely paced, quite complex and concentrated. Neither leads: they dance side-by-side. If you want to add another partner (this could get complicated), try grilled white fish, herbed roast chicken or grilled garlic shrimp.

NOTES

Fazi Battaglia Verdicchio dei Castelli di Jesi Classico 2012

★ ★ ★ ★

DOC VERDICCHIO DEI CASTELLI DI JESI CLASSICO

$11.60   (24422) XD

Fazi Battaglia packages its verdicchio in a distinctive bottle that looks a bit like an elongated Coca-Cola bottle. But the contents are much, much better. There are lovely fruit flavours and a touch of tanginess for good measure. With its fine balance and crisp texture, this wine is ideal for many kinds of seafood and white fish.

NOTES

Gabbiano 'Promessa' Pinot Grigio 2012

★ ★ ★ ★ ½

IGT DELLE VENEZIE $12.95   (77990) **XD**

The Castello di Gabbiano, home of this winery, is a thirteenth-century castle in Tuscany that is now also an elegant hotel. This pinot grigio from the Venice region is equally elegant. It shows lovely flavours that are fresh and substantial and a texture that's round, smooth and very refreshing. Dry and medium bodied, it's a wine you can sip as an aperitif or drink with rich or slightly spicy seafood, chicken, turkey or pork.

NOTES

....

....

....

....

Garolfoli Verdicchio dei Castelli di Jesi Classico Superiore 2012

★ ★ ★ ★ ½

DOC VERDICCHIO DEI CASTELLI DI JESI CLASSICO

$13.35 (277293) **XD**

This is a stylish white that you can enjoy on its own, as an aperitif or with many light seafood, fish, chicken or vegetable dishes. It delivers fresh, concentrated and focused flavours, lightened by the seam of bright acidity. It's very dry and medium weight.

NOTES

....

....

....

....

Masi Masianco 2012

★ ★ ★ ★ ½

IGT VENEZIE $15.00 (620773) **XD**

This is a very attractive blend of pinot grigio and verduzzo, with the verduzzo having been dried before being pressed to increase the intensity and complexity. The result is a white with real depth, while the pinot grigio contributes fresh fruitiness. Dry and medium weight, it's refreshing on its own or excellent paired with poultry, white fish, seafood and pork.

NOTES

....

....

....

....

Masi Modello delle Venezie Bianco 2012

★ ★ ★ ★

IGT BIANCO DELLE VENEZIE $10.95 (564674) **XD**

Made primarily with pinot grigio and ably assisted by some indigenous varieties, this is a straightforward, easy-drinking, fruity white that's nicely balanced to ensure a clean and crisp texture. This stands very well on its own, and it's quite versatile with food. Try it with spicy Asian dishes, roast chicken or pork or creamy pastas.

NOTES

Montalto Pinot Grigio 2013

★ ★ ★ ★

IGT TERRE SICILIANE $8.95   (73148) **XD**

This is a sibling to rival Montalto's Nero d'Avola/Cabernet Sauvignon (see page 183), and it's a reminder that Sicily used to be predominantly a white wine producer. This dry pinot grigio has lovely rich flavours that are nicely nuanced, and a tangy, fresh texture. It's an ideal partner for white fish and seafood, and it will also suit not-too-spicy sushi.

NOTES

Placido Pinot Grigio 2013

★ ★ ★ ★ ½

IGT TERRE SICILIANE $11.95   (588897) **D**

From northeastern Italy, this pinot grigio really stands out from many others. Drunk chilled but not too cold, it's almost elegant in style, with well-defined and focused flavours, good complexity and a finely integrated line of acidity that's both refreshing and soft. Dry and medium bodied, this is a great choice for many chicken, pork, fish and creamy pasta dishes.

NOTES

★ ★ ★ ★ ½   **Ruffino 'Lumina' Pinot Grigio 2013**

IGT DELLE VENEZIE $12.95 (589101) **XD**

This is quite an elegant pinot grigio for the price. The texture is smooth and mouth filling, but it retains freshness from the broad seam of acidity and the flavours are defined and focused. It's dry and medium bodied and it goes well with chicken, pork and mild cheeses.

NOTES

....

....

....

....

....

....

★ ★ ★ ★   **Ruffino Orvieto Classico 2013**

DOC ORVIETO CLASSICO $11.25   (31062) **D**

From vineyards near the beautiful town of Orvieto (the cathedral is shown on the label), this is a versatile dry white that's easy drinking on its own and a good match for lighter chicken, seafood and fish dishes, as well as for summer salads. The flavours show pure fruit, the acidity is refreshing and the balance very good.

NOTES

....

....

....

....

....

★ ★ ★ ★ ★   **Santa Margherita Pinot Grigio 2013**

DOC VALDADIGE $17.95 (106450) **D**

[Vintages Essential] This is a popular pinot grigio, and the secret of its success is its balance. Everything here harmonizes beautifully. It has enough of everything but not too much of anything. The acidity and fruit complement each other well and the flavours are neither too forward nor too restrained. It makes an excellent sipping wine before a meal, but also teams beautifully with food, especially seafood.

NOTES

....

....

....

....

Tommasi 'Le Rosse' Pinot Grigio 2013

★ ★ ★ ★

IGT DELLE VENEZIE $14.95 (270082) **D**

This well-made pinot grigio is from the region around Venice. The fruit is well concentrated and nicely layered with some ripe-sweetness at the core. The acidity shows through nicely, clean and fresh, making this a good choice for the table. With the hint of sweetness, this goes well with slightly spicy dishes, but it pairs with richer seafood and poultry, too.

NOTES

....

....

....

....

NEW ZEALAND

NEW ZEALAND IS A VERY SMALL PRODUCER of wine in global terms, but it made a big name for itself in the wine world in the 1990s with sauvignon blancs, especially those from Marlborough. They're still the core of the country's white wines, but chardonnay and other white varieties (and other regions) are definitely worth trying.

Alpine Valley Sauvignon Blanc 2012

★ ★ ★ ★

MARLBOROUGH $14.95 (241810) **XD**

The Marlborough wine region, New Zealand's biggest, lies in the north of
the South Island at the northern end of the Southern Alps, a snow-capped
range that runs all the way to the Central Otago wine region. This "savvy"
(as it's called in New Zealand) is bright and fresh, with quite dense and
pungent flavours and a juicy texture. It's a good choice for oysters, seafood
and white fish.

NOTES

....

....

....

....

Babich Sauvignon Blanc 2013

★ ★ ★ ★ ½

MARLBOROUGH $14.95 (620054) **XD**

The Babich family first cultivated vines early in the twentieth century near
Auckland, but the grapes for this wine come from much farther south,
the famed Marlborough region. It gives the wine its classic New Zealand
sauvignon flavours of exciting and pungent fruit. It's crisp and refreshing
with a smooth texture, and it goes wonderfully with warm goat cheese
salad or tomato and goat cheese quiche.

NOTES

....

....

....

....

Brancott 'B' Sauvignon Blanc 2011

★ ★ ★ ★ ★

MARLBOROUGH $19.95 (278689) **XD**

Here's a luscious sauvignon blanc from Marlborough, offering that great
one-two combination of ripe and complex fruit flavours and refreshing,
assertive acidity that makes you whimper for a plate of oysters or white
fish irrigated with lemon juice. Some Marlborough sauvignons are a bit
over the top in flavour intensity and acidity, but this one keeps everything
in the right place.

NOTES

....

....

....

....

Giesen Sauvignon Blanc 2013

NEW!
★ ★ ★ ★

MARLBOROUGH $17.95 (308270) **XD**

Another fine Marlborough sauvignon blanc, this one opening quite aromatically and following through to very good complexity on the palate. The flavours are well structured, carrying through consistently to the good finish, and they're supported by bright, fresh and clean acidity. Enjoy this with oysters, seafood, white fish or chicken dishes.

NOTES

Kate Radburnd 'Sun Kissed' Pinot Gris 2012

NEW!
★ ★ ★ ★ ½

HAWKE'S BAY $15.95 (359000) **D**

Look for really attractive and rich flavours in this lovely pinot gris from the east coast of the North Island. They're offset by a broad seam of clean, crisp acidity, giving this wine both weight and light juiciness. It's a great choice for rich dishes featuring chicken or pork, or richer seafoods such as scallops and lobster.

NOTES

Matua Valley Sauvignon Blanc 2013

★ ★ ★ ★ ★

HAWKE'S BAY $15.90 (619452) **XD**

If you're feeling a little jaded from your diet of Marlborough sauvignon blanc, try this one from Hawke's Bay, a region on New Zealand's North Island. It's a little different, a little fruitier, but it has the same style of plush and well-focused fruit flavours together with a full and refreshing texture. This is a great choice for grilled white fish or seafood, but try it with mussels steamed in white wine and garlic, too.

NOTES

Oyster Bay Sauvignon Blanc 2013

★ ★ ★ ★

MARLBOROUGH $18.95 (316570) **D**

[Vintages Essential] Here's a well-named wine. One of the classic food pairings with sauvignon blanc is freshly shucked oysters. The richness and acidity of the wine pick up the texture and brininess of the shellfish. This sauvignon blanc is quite lovely, with concentrated and pungent flavours that flow in on a tide that's crisp and refreshing. If you don't have fresh oysters to hand, try grilled white fish with fresh lemon.

NOTES

....

....

....

....

The People's Pinot Gris 2013

★ ★ ★ ★

HAWKE'S BAY $16.95 (240978) **XD**

Drawing on grapes from the Hawke's Bay wine region on the east coast of the North Island, this attractive, dry pinot gris goes well with well-seasoned or spicy dishes featuring seafood, white fish, chicken or pork. It has a smooth, quite plush texture, fruit that's sweet and solid from start to finish and very good fruit–acid balance.

NOTES

....

....

....

....

Stoneleigh Chardonnay 2013

★ ★ ★ ★

MARLBOROUGH $16.95 (288795) **XD**

From New Zealand's famous Marlborough region (best known for its sauvignon blancs) comes this delicious chardonnay. It's packed with ripe, fresh, vibrant fruit flavours that are concentrated and nuanced. They're accompanied by a rich, plush, refreshing texture that makes you think of food. It's dry and excellently balanced and goes very well with chicken, turkey or pork.

NOTES

....

....

....

....

★ ★ ★ ★

Stoneleigh Sauvignon Blanc 2013
MARLBOROUGH $17.55 (293043) **XD**

Marlborough gets more sunshine each year than almost any other part of New Zealand. Combine that with cool temperatures and you have perfect conditions for sauvignon blancs like this one. The fruit is ripe, sweet and pungent and it's undergirded with vibrant acidity. The result is a mouthwatering wine that sets you up for food. Seafood, shellfish and white fish are the classics, but try it with curried dishes, too.

NOTES
....
....
....
....

★ ★ ★ ★

Villa Maria 'Private Bin' Sauvignon Blanc 2012
MARLBOROUGH $16.95 (426601) **XD**

Villa Maria is a well-established New Zealand winery that I used to visit when I was a teenager living in Auckland. It's now transformed from a small local producer to a global exporter, thanks to wines like this sauvignon blanc. It delivers concentrated and well-defined flavours and a vibrant texture that picks up the natural acidity of the grape variety. It's an ideal choice for grilled white fish with a squeeze of lemon.

NOTES
....
....
....
....

★ ★ ★ ★

Whitecliff Sauvignon Blanc 2013
MARLBOROUGH $14.95 (610972) **XD**

This is a sauvignon blanc made in the classic Marlborough style that first put New Zealand on the wine map. The flavours are rich, pungent, complex and well defined, and there's a terrific seam of acidity running right through, contributing a clean, bright, zesty texture. It's a real palate cleanser and goes well with oysters or perhaps a tomato and goat cheese tart.

NOTES
....
....
....
....

★ ★ ★ ★ ½

Whitehaven Sauvignon Blanc 2013

MARLBOROUGH $18.95 (308288) XD

There's real fruit purity in this sauvignon. It has the rich complexity of many Marlborough sauvignons, but in this one the flavours are extraordinarily well defined and focused. They flow through the palate on a stream of bright, zesty acidity, and the flavours stay with you. It's a great choice for oysters and other white fish or seafood, especially with a drizzle of lemon juice.

NOTES

....

....

....

....

ONTARIO

SOME OF THE BEST WINES produced in Ontario are white. The cool growing conditions allow the grapes to ripen while achieving the levels of acidity they need to be crisp and refreshing. The most successful white varieties in the province are riesling, chardonnay, sauvignon blanc and gewürztraminer.

The initials VQA (Vintners Quality Alliance) on an Ontario wine label, followed by the name of a wine region, mean that the wine was made from grapes grown in that region and that the wine was tested and tasted for quality. The designated wine regions are Niagara Peninsula (and its sub-regions, such as Beamsville Bench and Niagara-on-the-Lake), Lake Erie North Shore, Pelee Island and Prince Edward County.

Non-VQA wines in the LCBO's Canada and Ontario sections are usually blends of a small percentage of Ontario wine and a high percentage of foreign wine. They are not included in this book.

NEW!
★★★★

Cattail Creek Riesling 2012
VQA NIAGARA PENINSULA $14.95 (241547) **M**

Although Cattail Creek has adopted feline themes for some of its wines, the name reflects the cattails that grow along Niagara's rivers. This is a luscious and well-balanced riesling in an off-dry style. The flavours are quite plush and complex and the acidity shows through well, cutting off most of the sweetness. It's a great choice for spicy, Asian cuisine.

NOTES

....

....

....

....

★★★★

Cave Spring 'Cave White' 2011
VQA NIAGARA PENINSULA $14.95 (305128) **XD**

Mainly chardonnay and sauvignon blanc, this is full of bright, fresh, fruity flavours that invite you to take one sip after another. It's dry with crisp acidity and is nicely balanced. This is the sort of white that's fine with or without food. Sip it on its own to perk up your appetite before dinner, or drink it with fish, chicken or seafood.

NOTES

....

....

....

....

....

★★★★

Cave Spring Chardonnay 2012
VQA NIAGARA PENINSULA $14.95 (228551) **XD**

Wine writers occasionally refer to the ABC movement, meaning Anything But Chardonnay, because, supposedly, many people are tired of chardonnay. This might change their minds. For the price, it's quite rich and stylish, with solid, mouth-filling fruit flavours, and it has a crisp, juicy texture. You'll enjoy this with lobster or with rich turkey, chicken and pork dishes.

NOTES

....

....

....

....

....

Cave Spring Dry Riesling 2012

★ ★ ★ ★ ½
VQA NIAGARA PENINSULA $14.95 (233635) **D**

Cave Spring quickly established a reputation for riesling, and it's still among the best producers in Ontario. Its rieslings tend to be stylish and complex, and they go beautifully with food. This one has a crisp and generous texture that's complemented by lovely nuanced fruit flavours. It's dry, refreshing and medium bodied. You can sip it as an aperitif, but it has the stuff to go with smoked chicken or pork tenderloin.

NOTES
....
....
....
....

Cave Spring 'Estate Bottled' Riesling 2012

★ ★ ★ ★ ★
VQA BEAMSVILLE BENCH $17.95 (286377) **D**

[Vintages Essential] Beamsville Bench is one of more than a dozen sub-appellations (or sub-regions) of the Niagara Peninsula appellation (wine region). It might be a bit confusing for consumers, but what's not confusing is this only-just-off-dry riesling. It delivers delicious, intense flavours on a texture that's brisk and clean, and it sets you up for food. So eat. Drink this with spicy seafood or smoked salmon.

NOTES
....
....
....
....

Cave Spring Riesling 2012

★ ★ ★ ★ ½
VQA NIAGARA PENINSULA $14.95 (234583) **MD**

Cave Spring winemaker Angelo Pavan hasn't lost his magic touch with riesling. This is a gorgeous off-dry example that displays rich, luscious, well-nuanced fruit flavours accompanied by a texture that's plush and mouth filling but also zesty and refreshing. It's the perfect wine for slightly spicy seafood, chicken and pork dishes, or for Thai or Indian food, whether vegetarian or meat-based.

NOTES
....
....
....
....

Cave Spring Sauvignon Blanc 2012

★ ★ ★ ★

VQA NIAGARA ESCARPMENT $15.95 (529933) **XD**

This is a lovely sauvignon blanc that goes well with grilled white fish
with a squeeze of lemon, freshly shucked oysters or fish and chips (but
avoid vinegar and stick to lemon). Made in a classic and popular style,
this sauvignon is dry and medium bodied, with a very refreshing
and zesty texture that lifts and enhances the well-defined and quite
concentrated flavours.

NOTES
....
....
....
....

Château des Charmes Aligoté 2012

★ ★ ★ ★

VQA ST. DAVID'S BENCH $13.95 (296848) **XD**

Aligoté is a little-known variety from Burgundy, where most of the
white wine is made from chardonnay. This Ontario aligoté has the crisp
texture and clean and refreshing aftertaste that's characteristic of the
variety, making it ideal for shellfish. It has rich and concentrated flavours
and a fairly round mouthfeel. Try it with roast chicken or grilled pork
chops, too.

NOTES
....
....
....
....

Château des Charmes 'Barrel Fermented' Chardonnay 2012

★ ★ ★ ★ ★

VQA NIAGARA-ON-THE-LAKE $13.95   (81653) **XD**

This is an especially delicious chardonnay in a style that I find irresistible
because it seamlessly combines weight and elegance. Look for plush
and well-defined fruit that's nicely complex and a round, smooth,
mouth-filling and refreshing texture. It shows terrific balance and is an
excellent choice for poultry, pork and even rich dishes like lobster and
seared scallops.

NOTES
....
....
....

Château des Charmes Sauvignon Blanc 2012

★ ★ ★ ★ ½

VQA ST. DAVID'S BENCH $14.95 (391300) **D**

St. David's Bench is a sub-appellation within the Niagara Peninsula wine region. This sauvignon blanc is really lovely, with lively, bright, but also solid and substantial flavours and a texture that's rich, refreshing and vibrant. It's dry and medium bodied and is an excellent wine to serve with grilled white fish and freshly squeezed lemon (or with fish and chips—but hold the vinegar).

NOTES

....
....
....
....
....

Coyote's Run Five Mile White 2012

★ ★ ★ ★

VQA NIAGARA PENINSULA $14.95 (195669) **D**

This is a blend of riesling, pinot gris and chardonnay, all varieties that do well in Ontario. It's slightly off-dry (off-dry-dry?), with bright and somewhat pungent flavours allied with a broad seam of vibrant acidity. It's the style of wine that's frequently suggested for spicy food, and this one goes well with sushi and Thai cuisine.

NOTES

....
....
....
....

Coyote's Run Pinot Gris/Pinot Blanc 2013

★ ★ ★ ★

VQA NIAGARA PENINSULA $15.95 (112144) **XD**

This is a blend of two varieties often associated with Alsace. Here they make for a dry and fruity white with bright but serious flavours holding solid right through the palate. The acidity is well calibrated, making this a versatile wine. You can happily sip it on its own or pair it with chicken, pork, seafood or white fish, or with many lightly spicy Asian dishes.

NOTES

....
....
....
....
....

Creekside Pinot Grigio 2012

★ ★ ★ ★

VQA NIAGARA PENINSULA $14.95   (83196) **XD**

This is a very attractive pinot grigio with well-defined and complex flavours and a great clean, crisp, refreshing texture. There's a pink tinge to the wine from the grape skins which are often a greyish-pink colour. It's not as fruity as many pinot grigios, and the texture makes it an excellent choice for many foods. Try it with chicken, pork and shellfish (like mussels steamed in white wine).

NOTES

....

....

....

....

....

Creekside Sauvignon Blanc 2012

★ ★ ★ ★ ½

VQA NIAGARA PENINSULA $13.95 (620724) **XD**

This is a vibrant, crisp sauvignon with persistent fresh and nicely complex flavours. The acidity plays a great role here and contributes to making the wine versatile at the table. Drink it with the usual sauvignon suspects (oysters, seafood, white fish, goat cheese) but try it with medium-hot curries or fish and chips.

NOTES

....

....

....

....

Earth & Sky Riesling 2012

NEW!
★ ★ ★ ★ ½

VQA NIAGARA PENINSULA $14.95   (343350) **D**

Made by Château des Charmes, this is a dry riesling that speaks quality all the way through. There's the slightest hint of sweetness that might just be fruitiness, and the flavours are nuanced and focused right through. They're supported by bracing and refreshing acidity, and the whole is well integrated. This riesling pairs with many poultry and pork dishes, as well as with seafood and smoked salmon.

NOTES

....

....

....

....

★ ★ ★ ★ **Fielding Estate Fireside White 2012**

VQA NIAGARA PENINSULA $13.95 (303040) **M**

An interesting blend of riesling, gewürzrtraminer, pinot gris and chardonnay, this wine shows both complexity and vibrancy. The tension is evident in the flavours—which are complex and sweet-centred—and the full but clean and crisp texture. The viognier/pinot gris pushes toward spicy dishes, and the riesling and chardonnay toward roast chicken and grilled fish. They all work. You decide.

NOTES

....

....

....

....

....

★ ★ ★ ★ **Fielding Estate Pinot Gris 2012**

VQA NIAGARA PENINSULA $18.95 (223610) **D**

There's a little sweetness here, but don't avoid this if your preference is for dry wines. The flavour complexity and well-calibrated acidity give the wine a dry feel, and it ends quite astringently. Medium bodied and quite elegant, this is a great choice for spicy seafood, shellfish or poultry dishes, whether or not they're Asian-inspired.

NOTES

....

....

....

....

....

★ ★ ★ ★ **Fielding Estate Riesling 2012**

VQA NIAGARA PENINSULA $15.95 (146761) **M**

Fielding's logo is a Muskoka chair, and this is the kind of wine you want when you kick back to relax. It's off-dry with plenty of acidity to smooth things out, and it has a crisp, clean feel in your mouth. Sip it on its own, serve it as an aperitif or drink it with spicy Asian dishes or melon and prosciutto.

NOTES

....

....

....

....

Fielding Estate White Conception 2012

NEW!
★ ★ ★ ★

VQA NIAGARA PENINSULA $18.95 (203737) **D**

White Conception is a blend of chardonnay (51 percent), viognier (39 percent) and sauvignon blanc (10 percent). It's an easy-drinking, but serious wine that shows well-defined ripe fruit flavours throughout, and a spine of clean, refreshing acidity that dries out the fruit. The balance is well done, and it's a good choice for many poultry, pork, white fish and seafood dishes.

NOTES

....
....
....
....
....

Flat Rock Twisted 2013

NEW!
★ ★ ★ ★ ½

VQA NIAGARA PENINSULA $16.95 (1578) **D**

[Vintages Essential] This blend of riesling, gewürztraminer and chardonnay is drier that most similar combinations, thanks to the fresh acidity that accompanies the fruit. The flavours are generous but nicely nuanced and the texture is crisp and clean. It's a natural for many Asian dishes with sweet spices, and goes well with many pork and chicken dishes, too.

NOTES

....
....
....
....

G. Marquis 'The Red Line' Pinot Grigio 2012

NEW!
★ ★ ★ ★

VQA NIAGARA PENINSULA $11.95 (276501) **XD**

This is a well-made, attractive, dry pinot grigio that you can enjoy on its own or with many dishes that feature chicken, turkey, pork or white fish. The flavours are generous and well focused from start to finish, and they're carried through the palate on a seam of acidity that's bright and clean.

NOTES

....
....
....
....
....

Henry of Pelham Chardonnay 2012

★ ★ ★ ★ ½

VQA NIAGARA PENINSULA $13.95 (291211) **XD**

This wine was made and aged in stainless steel to preserve the purity of
the fruit flavours. It worked. This is just a very well-made wine—nothing
to make you run screaming into the street, but a wine to enjoy. The sweet
and ripe flavours are substantial but nuanced and delicate, and the texture
is clean and refreshing. It's a natural for roast chicken or pork and for a
simple white fish dish.

NOTES

....

....

....

....

Henry of Pelham Riesling 2013

★ ★ ★ ★ ½

VQA NIAGARA PENINSULA $13.95 (268375) **D**

Riesling has led the way with screw caps—first in New Zealand and
Australia, then elsewhere. The seal captures the freshness you want in the
variety, and Henry of Pelham delivers. This dry riesling is packed with
delicious flavour together with a round and crisp, clean texture. It's a great
choice for sipping on the deck or before dinner, but it's also excellent with
fish, seafood, chicken or pork dishes.

NOTES

....

....

....

....

Henry of Pelham Sauvignon Blanc 2013

★ ★ ★ ★

VQA NIAGARA PENINSULA $14.95 (430546) **XD**

This very attractive sauvignon blanc has all the zesty crispness of texture
and brightness of fruit you look for in this variety, without the pungency
that often overpowers food. The flavours are lively and textured, it's dry
and medium bodied, and it goes well with shellfish, seafood or grilled or
pan-fried white fish with fresh lemon.

NOTES

....

....

....

....

....

Inniskillin Riesling 2011

★ ★ ★ ★

VQA NIAGARA PENINSULA $12.95   (83790) **D**

This is a well-made dry riesling that goes well with a range of food; try it with white fish and seafood, roast chicken, pork or turkey or summer salads. It's dry, with a crisp, vibrant texture, and the acidity holds up the fresh, vibrant flavours well. They're nicely concentrated and persist right through the palate.

NOTES

....

....

....

....

....

Inniskillin Unoaked Chardonnay 2011

★ ★ ★ ★

VQA NIAGARA PENINSULA $12.95   (66266) **XD**

Inniskillin Winery was named for Inniskillin Farm, which after the War of 1812 was a land grant to a colonel in the Inniskilling Fusiliers. This is a well-made chardonnay with well-defined flavours. It's dry with a medium body and has a solid and very refreshing texture—the sort of wine you can sip on its own in the afternoon or enjoy with roast or grilled chicken, white fish, seafood or cream-based pasta dishes.

NOTES

....

....

....

....

Jackson-Triggs Reserve Gewürztraminer 2012

★ ★ ★ ★

VQA NIAGARA PENINSULA $12.95   (526269) **D**

This gewürztraminer is made in a very attractive style—not too blowsy, but with flavours that are nicely tuned and have a certain delicacy, while the texture is both mouth filling and spicy. The acidity comes through well and makes this surprisingly refreshing for the variety. Drink it with spicy seafood or with Thai dishes.

NOTES

....

....

....

....

....

Jackson-Triggs Reserve Riesling 2012

★ ★ ★ ★ ½

VQA NIAGARA PENINSULA $12.95 (526277) **M**

This is a lovely riesling just bursting with rich, ripe fruit. There's good concentration and complexity, and the fruit is supported by vibrant acidity that lends the wine a juicy texture. It's off-dry, with the acidity offsetting the sugar nicely. This is a great choice for spicy dishes, but it's refreshing enough that you can enjoy it on its own, too.

NOTES

....
....
....
....
....

NEW!

★ ★ ★ ★ ½

Kacaba Unoaked Chardonnay 2013

VQA NIAGARA PENINSULA $14.95 (326975) **D**

This is a lovely crisp chardonnay that delivers very attractive flavours and makes a versatile white for the table. The fruit is ripe-sweet at the core, with good complexity, and the acidity is fresh, clean and pushes to the verge of juiciness. It's dry and harmonious and makes a very good partner for many poultry, pork and white fish dishes.

NOTES

....
....
....
....
....

Mike Weir Chardonnay 2012

★ ★ ★ ★

VQA NIAGARA PENINSULA $14.95 (00026) **XD**

Yes, that is product code number 26, not Mike's score around nine holes. The chardonnay plays well right through the course. It drives off with quite intense and decently complex flavours and hits the fairway with a taut texture offset by good acidity. It's as dry as a summer day on the links, and medium bodied. You'll be popular putting this out when you're serving roast chicken or grilled salmon.

NOTES

....
....
....
....

Peninsula Ridge 'Inox' Unoaked Chardonnay 2012

★ ★ ★ ★ ½

VQA NIAGARA PENINSULA $13.95 (594200) **XD**

This chardonnay spends no time at all in oak barrels. "Inox" refers to the stainless steel tanks that the wine is made in, and the purpose of using stainless steel is to present the fruit flavours and texture without any oak influence. What you get here are beautifully clean, pure flavours and excellent balance. It's almost full bodied, with a generous texture, and pairs well with pork, chicken and white fish.

NOTES

....

....

....

....

Peninsula Ridge Sauvignon Blanc 2012

★ ★ ★ ★ ½

VQA NIAGARA PENINSULA $13.95   (53678) **XD**

Peninsula Ridge was the first winery where I tasted an Ontario sauvignon blanc I thought was stunning. It's vintage variable, but this one is full of sauvignon character, with clean and pungent fruit flavours, a fairly full texture that's quite high in refreshing acidity and a long, clean finish. Drink it with the usual suspects—freshly-shucked oysters—or with battered white fish, chips and tartar sauce.

NOTES

....

....

....

....

Reif Riesling 2012

★ ★ ★ ★

VQA NIAGARA RIVER $12.95   (111799) **D**

This is a very attractive riesling in a dry style but showing plenty of fruit ripeness in the flavours. They're paired with a good line of clean and refreshing acidity, making this a versatile white for sipping on its own or at the table. Drink it on its own or with roast pork, white fish, seafood or mildly spiced Asian dishes.

NOTES

....

....

....

....

....

Southbrook 'Connect' Organic White 2013
★ ★ ★ ★
VQA ONTARIO $14.95 (249078) **M**

This attractive off-dry blend of vidal and riesling has plenty of fruit, good focus and intensity, along with the acidity to give it a bright and crisp texture. It's easy drinking on its own and a very good option for sushi and other spicy Asian dishes.

NOTES

Strewn Gewürztraminer 2012
★ ★ ★ ★
VQA NIAGARA PENINSULA $12.95 (65359) **D**

Gewürztraminer is an underappreciated variety (maybe because it looks difficult to pronounce), which is a pity, because it does well in Niagara. This example shows good, understated flavours with concentration and modest complexity, with fresh acidity and the telltale (and attractive) hint of bitterness at the end. Drink it with well-seasoned roast chicken and pork.

NOTES

Strewn 'Two Vines' Riesling/Gewürztraminer 2012
★ ★ ★ ★
VQA NIAGARA PENINSULA $11.95 (467662) **D**

The name of this winery has no relation to wine, location or the owners' names. They were simply looking for a word that was pithy and neutral, and "strewn" fitted the bill. This off-dry blend combines the rich flavours of gewürztraminer and the zestiness of riesling. It makes a great aperitif to whet your appetite, or a partner with spicy—possibly Asian-inspired—dishes of seafood, chicken or pork.

NOTES

★ ★ ★ ★

Trius Riesling 2012

VQA NIAGARA PENINSULA $13.95 (303792) **D**

With so many good-quality and good-value rieslings around—like this one—it's a pity that the variety isn't more popular. Maybe it's because many people still associate it with older-style sweet wines. Ontario produces many fabulous rieslings. This one is just slightly off-dry, full of lovely, vibrant fruit flavours, and it has a lively, crisp texture. It's medium bodied and an excellent choice for rich seafood, chicken or pork dishes.

NOTES

....

....

....

NEW!
★ ★ ★ ★ ½

Vineland Estates Semi-Dry Riesling 2012

VQA NIAGARA PENINSULA $13.95 (232033) **D**

It's called "semi-dry," another way of saying "off-dry," but this is clearly on the dry side. There's just a hint of sweetness in the rich, generous fruit, which is offset by the bright and clean acidity that gives the wine a lovely juicy texture. This is a wine that is very easy to drink on its own, but which also goes well with many chicken, turkey and pork dishes.

NOTES

....

....

....

....

....

OREGON

OREGON IS A SIGNIFICANT producer of wine, and is well known for its pinot noirs. But it also makes many fine whites. Watch the biweekly Vintages releases for other Oregon wines.

Firesteed Pinot Gris 2012

OREGON $17.80 (323808) **D**

This is a nicely made pinot gris that delivers plenty of plush, ripe-sweet flavours that are consistent from attack to finish. They're underpinned by a platform of fresh acidity that contributes crispness and versatile food-friendliness to the texture. You can drink this with a wide range of dishes, from white fish to poultry to pork.

NOTES

....

....

....

....

PORTUGAL

PORTUGAL DOESN'T SHOW VERY brightly on the radar of Ontario wine drinkers, and when it does, it's more for the reds than the whites. The best-known Portuguese white is Vinho Verde, a fruity, spritzy wine that's meant to be drunk young, but there are other interesting whites made from indigenous grapes.

Portugal's official wine regions are indicated by DOC (*Denominação de Origem Controlada*) on the label.

★ ★ ★ ★

Quinta da Aveleda Vinho Verde 2012

DOC VINHO VERDE $9.95   (89995) **XD**

I can see sipping this before a meal throughout the year, or while sitting on the deck or lounging at the cottage in the summer. It's a simple, light white with a low alcohol level of 11.5 percent (just what you need in the summer), sweet fruit flavours and a light spritziness that adds to its refreshing, palate-cleansing character. You can also enjoy it with spicy appetizers.

NOTES

....

....

....

....

SOUTH AFRICA

SOUTH AFRICA'S WINE REGIONS are mostly warm, which makes you think of red wine. But they produce many very good whites, too. The most popular variety used to be chenin blanc, but over the last ten years others (especially chardonnay and sauvignon blanc) have become more important.

Wines from official South African wine regions are called Wines of Origin. In this list, the letters "WO" followed by a region indicate where the wine is from.

★ ★ ★ ★ The Beachhouse Sauvignon Blanc/Semillon 2013
WO WESTERN CAPE $9.95 (122390) **D**

If you're looking for a well-made, easy-drinking white, this might well be it. It shows the solid, bright flavours and crispness of sauvignon blanc and the rounder, more substantial weight of semillon, all nicely integrated. You can enjoy it on its own, but it goes well with many seafood and white fish dishes, as well as not-too-hot curries and Asian dishes.

NOTES

....

....

....

....

....

★ ★ ★ ★ Boschendal 'The Pavillion' Chenin Blanc/Viognier 2013
WO WESTERN CAPE $10.95 (281311) **XD**

Look for quite plush and rich fruit in this blend, with a core of sweet ripeness and nicely layered flavours. The acidity and fruit are in a good relationship, with the acidity keeping the richness of the fruit in check and giving the wine a crisp, fresh texture. Drink it with richer seafood, poultry and pork dishes.

NOTES

....

....

....

....

....

NEW!
★ ★ ★ ★ Douglas Green Sauvignon Blanc 2013
WO WESTERN CAPE $10.95 (367821) **XD**

For an overall warm-climate country, South Africa turns out a surprising number of superior sauvignons. This one delivers effectively across the board. The flavours are well-defined and nicely complex, and they're complemented by clean, brisk acidity. It's an easy choice for white fish and poultry.

NOTES

....

....

....

....

....

Durbanville Hills Sauvignon Blanc 2013

★ ★ ★ ★

WO DURBANVILLE $11.95 (22251) **XD**

This dry and medium-bodied sauvignon blanc will stand its ground against many that are significantly higher priced. It delivers concentrated flavours that are vibrant and substantial and a texture that's mouth filling, smooth and very refreshing. It's a good choice when you're eating grilled white fish or seafood with fresh lemon, or lemon chicken.

NOTES

....
....
....
....
....

Goats do Roam White 2013

★ ★ ★ ★ ½

WO COASTAL REGION $11.95 (237313) **XD**

Not only does this winery have a herd of goats, the name is also a play on côtes du Rhône, the French wine region. And, as it happens, this dry, medium-weight wine is made from grape varieties typical to that region: viognier (67 percent), roussanne (19 percent) and grenache blanc (14 percent). Look for great depth of flavour here, with good complexity, and a refreshing and juicy texture. It's great with poultry, pork and rich seafood dishes.

NOTES

....
....
....

NEW!
★ ★ ★ ★

KWV 'Contemporary Collection' Chenin Blanc 2013

WO WESTERN CAPE $9.45 (18689) **D**

Two big South African names here: KWV is the country's largest wine producer, and chenin blanc is the country's most widely planted grape variety. This is not a complicated white, but it's definitely a crowd-pleaser in the best sense. It delivers lovely flavours, with some complexity and a bright, fresh texture. You can drink this on its own, or pair it with simple fish, seafood, chicken and pork dishes.

NOTES

....
....
....

★ ★ ★ ★ **Nederburg 'The Winemaster's Reserve' Sauvignon Blanc 2013**

WO WESTERN CAPE $11.45 (382713) **XD**

Nederburg is an established (over two centuries old) and big (production is about 13 million bottles a year) South African wine producer. Although, for wineries, age is sometimes seen as an advantage but size a problem, the company keeps quality up. This sauvignon blanc is zesty and refreshing, with good, clean flavours. It's made for food, so pair it with seafood or fish with a squeeze of lemon.

NOTES

....

....

....

★ ★ ★ ★ ½ **Petit Chenin Blanc 2013**

WO STELLENBOSCH $12.95 (266106) **XD**

What a great combination: this is made from South Africa's signature white variety by one of the country's great winemakers, Ken Forrester. Everything's in place here: flavours that are concentrated, focused and defined, a texture that's fresh and solid. This is fruity but serious. It goes well with poultry and pork and easily extends to slightly spicy Asian cuisine.

NOTES

....

....

....

....

★ ★ ★ ★ **Two Oceans Sauvignon Blanc 2013**

WO WESTERN CAPE $10.25 (340380) **D**

The two oceans involved here are the Atlantic and the Indian, and where they meet (the point shifts seasonally) off South Africa's coast, breezes develop that blow onto the land and cool the vines. This is an attractive sauvignon blanc, with well-defined and nicely concentrated flavours and a crisp, clean texture. Enjoy it with warm goat cheese salad or with white fish or seafood.

NOTES

....

....

....

....

Waka Waka Sauvignon Blanc 2013

★ ★ ★ ★

WO PAARL $12.95 (266494) **XD**

The grapes used for this wine were grown on bush vines without supports, unlike most vines that are trained along trellises or wires. The wine is full of flavour, with good complexity and depth, and the acidity is crisp and bright. This is a very attractive sauvignon blanc that goes well with seafood, shellfish and white fish, and pairs nicely with curries, too.

NOTES

....

....

....

....

The Wolftrap White 2012

★ ★ ★ ★ ★

WO FRANSCHHOEK $13.95   (292532) **D**

This terrific blend of viognier, chenin blanc and grenache blanc is made by iconic producer Boekenhoutskloof. That's a mouthful, and so is this wine—a mouthful of plush, ripe-sweet fruit that's concentrated, layered and consistent. It's supported by a broad seam of fresh acidity that gives it some juiciness. Drink it with pork or chicken, or with many spicy dishes.

NOTES

....

....

....

....

SPAIN

SPAIN IS BEST KNOWN for its red wines, its sherry (see page 246) and its sparkling wine, cava (see page 227). Much of the white table wine that Spain produces is consumed locally and never reaches international markets. However, that's changing as some of the larger wineries, like Torres, occasionally make white wines available in the LCBO's Vintages section. Hopefully some of these will eventually make their way to the General Purchase List.

The initials DO (*Denominación de Origen*) indicate a wine from one of Spain's designated wine regions. A higher-quality level, DOC (*Denominación de Origen Calificada*) has been awarded to only two regions: Rioja and Priorat.

Marqués de Riscal 2013

★ ★ ★ ★

DO RUEDA $13.00   (36822) **XD**

This is an attractive blend that's excellent for sipping on the patio or
before a meal. Serve it with grilled or pan-fried white fish or roast chicken.
It's dry and medium bodied, with attractive and fairly concentrated
fruit flavours. The texture is appealing, with richness from the fruit
complemented by a refreshing crispness that makes it great by itself or
with food.

NOTES

....

....

....

....

NEW!

★ ★ ★ ★   ### Torres 'Vina Esmeralda' 2012

DO CATALUNYA $14.95   (113696) **D**

Made from moscatel and gewürztraminer, this is a fruity, spicy, off-
dry white that you can easily enjoy on its own or take to the table. It's
especially well suited to Asian cuisine, spicy or well-seasoned vegetables,
poultry or pork. It has a distinctly juicy texture, thanks to the bright
acidity that underlies the concentrated and consistent fruit flavour.

NOTES

....

....

....

....

WASHINGTON

THE STATE OF WASHINGTON is an important wine-producing region that's especially well known for merlots. Few Washington wines appear on LCBO shelves, but some are released from time to time by Vintages.

14 Hands 'Hot to Trot' White Blend 2011

★ ★ ★ ★

WASHINGTON STATE $15.40 (280859) **D**

Named for the small wild horses that used to roam the Columbia Valley, this is a blend of mainly chardonnay, pinot gris and semillon. There's a pretty touch of sweetness on the palate, giving character to flavours that are forward, concentrated and well defined. The acidity shines through to freshen it. It's the sort of wine you can as happily sip on its own or bring to the table, where you can serve it with richer seafood, fish and poultry dishes.

NOTES

....

....

....

....

ARGENTINA

ARGENTINA IS THE WORLD's fifth-largest wine producer, but it began to make its mark on the world wine scene only a few years ago. Although we see more and more quality and good-value wines from there, we haven't seen half of what Argentina can do. Wine producers (mostly located in the sprawling Mendoza region) make superlative reds and whites, and it's the reds that are starting to get attention. Malbec, a red grape native to southwest France, has become Argentina's signature variety. Made in big and robust styles, the wine is a natural for beef, which just happens to be another of Argentina's major products. But cabernet sauvignons and other reds can be just as impressive.

Alamos Cabernet Sauvignon 2012

★ ★ ★ ★

MENDOZA $13.95 (295105) **D**

Made from grapes growing in the foothills of the Andes, this shows the ripeness that cabernet sauvignon achieves in the sunny warmth. The flavours are robust, intense and well layered, and a seam of good, clean acidity gives the wine tanginess. This is definitely for hearty red meats like grilled steak and lamb.

NOTES

....
....
....
....
....

Argento Bonarda 2012

★ ★ ★ ★

MENDOZA $9.95 (292458) **D**

Bonarda is Argentina's second most–widely grown grape variety (after malbec), and it makes intensely flavoured and juicy wines like this. The flavours are intense and defined, and the acidity comes through well to contribute the juiciness. The tannins are drying but easygoing. This is excellent for grilled red meats, burgers and seasoned sausages.

NOTES

....
....
....
....

Catena Malbec 2011

★ ★ ★ ★ ½

MENDOZA $19.95 (478727) **D**

[Vintages Essential] Malbec from Argentina hit the wine world a bit like Australian shiraz did in the 1990s, and they often share a popular style: intense fruit flavours, generous texture and easygoing acidity. This malbec from Catena is a cut above many others. It delivers structure and balance along with power and intensity. It's a great wine for full-flavoured grilled red meats.

NOTES

....
....
....
....
....

★ ★ ★

FuZion 'Alta' Reserva Cabernet Sauvignon 2012

MENDOZA $9.95 (207357) **D**

Although known worldwide for malbec, Argentina produces exceptional cabernet sauvignon. This is a very well-priced, entry-level example, but it delivers well across the board. It's lively and fresh, carries ripe and sweet fruit with some complexity, and has modest tannins. It's a very good choice for burgers, ribs and all kinds of red meat, grilled or braised.

NOTES

....
....
....
....
....

★ ★ ★

FuZion 'Orgánico' Malbec/Cabernet 2013

MENDOZA $12.95 (127456) **D**

There are so many wines in the FuZion range that it can cause confusion. Look for this one, though, as it delivers good quality across the board. It's full of ripe fruit, as you'd expect, and it's layered, plush and, importantly, supported by a seam of fresh acidity. The tannins are moderate, and this goes well with Argentina's main meat: grilled beef.

NOTES

....
....
....
....
....

★ ★ ★ ★ ½

Graffigna 'Centenario' Reserve Malbec 2011

SAN JUAN $13.95 (230474) **XD**

San Juan, where the grapes for this wine grow, lies just a couple of hours' drive north of Mendoza, Argentina's main wine-producing region. This is a malbec that shows a lot of character for the price. Look for concentrated flavours that have complexity and structure, paired with the acidity to contribute a juicy texture. It's a good choice for grilled red meats and many other full-flavoured dishes.

NOTES

....
....
....
....

Graffigna 'Centenario' Reserve Shiraz 2011

★ ★ ★ ★

SAN JUAN $13.95   (164731) **D**

After stealing some of the popular red market with malbec, maybe Argentina will give Australia a run for its money with shiraz, too. This gutsy example, from the San Juan region (where more shiraz than malbec is planted), shows plush, full-on fruit, good fruit–acid balance and a fleshy, tangy texture. It's a great buy for burgers, ribs and red meats from the barbecue in summer or the grill in winter.

NOTES

....

....

....

....

Kaiken Reserva Malbec 2011

★ ★ ★ ★

MENDOZA $14.95   (58339) **XD**

[Vintages Essential] With so many Argentine malbecs available, the choice can be confusing. This is a pretty easy one, though. You'll find plenty of ripe fruit flavours, a fairly smooth texture, light tannins and a line of fresh acidity to keep it all honest. It's dry and a good choice for grilled red meats and burgers.

NOTES

....

....

....

....

La Linda Syrah 2012

★ ★ ★ ★

MENDOZA $11.95   (223651) **XD**

La Linda is a brand of Luigi Bosca, a well-known Argentine producer. This is an affordable syrah that's a break from the ocean of merlot on the LCBO's shelves. Look for well-concentrated and focused flavours with some complexity, and a round and tangy texture. You can't go wrong pouring this syrah with red meats and many rich poultry dishes.

NOTES

....

....

....

....

NEW!
★ ★ ★ ★

La Mascota Cabernet Sauvignon 2011

MENDOZA $14.40 (292110) **D**

Argentina produces many fine cabernet sauvignons, which go as well
with the country's beef-heavy diet as the better-known malbecs. This full-
bodied cabernet is quite rich, with plush and concentrated flavours and
a generous and smooth texture. It has enough acidity to suit it to food,
though, and it's a natural for well-seasoned red meats.

NOTES
....
....
....
....
....

★ ★ ★ ★ ½

La Posta 'Tinto' Red Blend 2013

MENDOZA $13.85 (269860) **D**

This is a dry blend of malbec (60 percent) with equal parts bonarda
and syrah. The fruit is bright and ripe, and it's harnessed to a seam of
refreshing acidity that gives the wine some very attractive juiciness. The
tannins are very drying and leave an astringent feeling, but each sip cleans
it up. This is a great choice for many styles of food, from grilled red meats
to pasta and hearty stews.

NOTES
....
....
....
....

★ ★ ★ ★ ★

Luigi Bosca Malbec 2011

MENDOZA $17.95 (79293) **XD**

[Vintages Essential] This malbec punches above its weight and is several
cuts above many others at this and higher prices. Look for concentrated
fruit with weight, structure and attractive layering, and a good seam
of acidity that lightens its impact. The tannins are ripe and drying.
Everything holds together well, and this is a great choice for grilled red
meats. It will age, too; you can safely hang on to it through 2018.

NOTES
....
....
....
....

Masi Passo Doble 2011

★ ★ ★ ★

TUPUNGATO $13.95 (620880) **XD**

This is a blend of the malbec and corvina varieties for which the corvina grapes have been dried before being pressed. Drying eliminates some of the water so that the grapes have more concentrated and complex flavours. You can taste it in this wine, which shows intense and well-focused flavours and a rich, tangy texture. It goes well with a wide range of red meat dishes and hearty stews of all kinds.

NOTES

....

....

....

....

Misterio Malbec 2012

★ ★ ★ ★

MENDOZA $9.95   (28803) **XD**

This 100 percent malbec gets four months' aging in oak casks. The back label says it's "full of mystery," but I find it full of plush, ripe fruit flavours that are nicely balanced. It's dry and medium bodied and has a tangy texture. It's a very affordable choice for grilled red meats—great when you're having a crowd for a barbecue.

NOTES

....

....

....

....

Norton Cabernet Sauvignon 2012

★ ★ ★ ★

MENDOZA $11.00 (589556) **XD**

Norton was founded by a British engineer who went to Argentina in the 1880s to build a railroad, married an Argentine woman and received land as a present from her father. He planted the land in grapes and now Norton is one of Argentina's largest wineries. This cabernet is full of ripe fruit, modestly complex and well balanced with fresh acidity. It's a great choice for burgers, pizzas and red meat dishes.

NOTES

....

....

....

....

....

★ ★ ★ ★ ½

Pascual Toso 'Limited Edition' Malbec 2011

MENDOZA $15.95 (162610) **D**

This is a step or two above many malbecs at this price. It has all the rich flavour that you expect of Argentine malbec, but the integration and harmony of the components are notable. The fruit is ripe and focused, the acidity well calibrated and the tannins supple. Dry and medium bodied, it's a great choice for anything from a gourmet burger to a seasoned rack of lamb.

NOTES

....
....
....
....
....

★ ★ ★ ★

Tilia Malbec 2013

MENDOZA $12.95 (160945) **XD**

This Argentine malbec is a cut above many of the rest at this price point. It has all the rich, concentrated flavours that you expect of malbec, but it adds very good degrees of complexity, good structure and nice fruit–acid balance. It's great with hearty stews and red meats, especially with beef, Argentina's meat of choice.

NOTES

....
....
....
....
....

★ ★ ★ ★

Trapiche Malbec 2013

MENDOZA $9.95 (501551) **D**

This is a very dry red that shows focused, solid fruit from start to finish. The complexity is good and the balance with the fresh acidity is well done. The tannins are easygoing, and this very drinkable (and affordable) malbec makes a great partner for red meats, burgers and pizzas.

NOTES

....
....
....
....
....

Trapiche Reserve Syrah 2012

★ ★ ★ ★

MENDOZA $11.95 (222281) **XD**

What gives this syrah added points is that it's well balanced. So many wines at this price are full of fruit and short on almost everything else, but here you get a tangy, fresh texture from the acidity and astringent dryness from the tannins. It's medium bodied and it goes well with red meat dishes generally, but also with pork and poultry.

NOTES

....
....
....
....
....
....

Trivento 'Special Selection' Malbec 2012

NEW!
★ ★ ★ ★

MENDOZA $11.95 (160994) **D**

This is a "fair trade" malbec, made from grapes purchased from a group of small-farm owners. You'll find it has all the qualities you look for in a malbec at this price range, and then some. The fruit is solid right through the palate, it has decent complexity, and it's well balanced with the acidity. It's an obvious choice for grilled red meats.

NOTES

....
....
....
....
....

Urban Uco Malbec-Tempranillo 2012

NEW!
★ ★ ★ ★

UCO VALLEY $13.70 (308254) **D**

This is from one of the higher-altitude areas of Argentina, where the vines grow at over a thousand metres above sea level. They benefit from sunny days and cool nights, and the ripe fruit and crisp, clean acidity in this wine are suggestive of the growing conditions. Half malbec and half tempranillo, it's full of attractive, layered flavours with easygoing tannins. Enjoy it with red meats, burgers and grilled sausages.

NOTES

....
....
....

AUSTRALIA

AUSTRALIA IS A REAL POWERHOUSE for red wine, and Australian shiraz dominated New World red wine exports for years. But although shiraz is king, other red varieties are very important, notably cabernet sauvignon, merlot and pinot noir.

The most common geographical designation for Australian wine is South Eastern Australia. This isn't a state but a mega-zone that includes more than 90 percent of the country's wine production and most of its wine regions. The best-known smaller regions include Barossa Valley and McLaren Vale, both of which are represented in this list.

Angus the Bull Cabernet Sauvignon 2011

★ ★ ★ ★ ½

SOUTH EASTERN AUSTRALIA $19.95 (602615) **XD**

Now and again, a wine stands out from the herd, and Angus is one of them. It delivers generous, concentrated flavours that are complex and ripe, but well on this side of the fence that separates ripe from jammy. Full bodied and juicy with relaxed tannins, it's a great partner for . . . beef, of course. But don't be cowed by this, and don't let me steer you away from serving Angus with other red meats.

NOTES

....
....
....
....

d'Arenberg 'The Stump Jump' Grenache/Shiraz/Mourvèdre 2011

★ ★ ★ ★

MCLAREN VALE $14.95 (173294) **XD**

Named for a plough that used to jump over difficult roots, this blend (known as GSM) delivers nicely concentrated fruit that's layered and solid right through, with a seam of acidity that makes the wine quite juicy and friendly toward any food in its vicinity. For the most part it gravitates toward burgers, grilled veal and pork, and well-seasoned snarlers, as sausages are sometimes known where this wine comes from.

NOTES

....
....
....
....

Fifth Leg 'Old Dog New Tricks' Shiraz 2012

★ ★ ★ ★

WESTERN AUSTRALIA $15.95 (281345) **D**

My daughter is a certified dog trainer (pupwellness.com), and she assures me you can teach an old dog new tricks. This is a very attractive shiraz—not in your face like a big untrained puppy, but restrained, as the acidity keeps the fruit on a leash. Dry and moderately tannic, it's a very good wine to be lapped up with grilled red meats and burgers.

NOTES

....
....
....
....

★ ★ ★ ★

Fifth Leg Shiraz/Merlot/Cabernet Sauvignon 2012
WESTERN AUSTRALIA $16.00 (212605) **XD**

This is a terrific blend. It shows loads of plush, intense fruit that's consistent right through the palate, and brings it into harmony and balance with a seam of fresh acidity that lightens the intensity. The tannins are easygoing. This is wine you can enjoy with well-seasoned grilled and braised red meats.

NOTES

....
....
....
....
....

NEW!
★ ★ ★ ★ ★

Fowles 'Are you Game?' Shiraz 2012
VICTORIA $16.95 (327320) **XD**

Like its chardonnay sibling, this is designed to go with game. The buck on the front label suggests one pairing, but you can go domesticated, too, and drink this with a wide range of red meats. This is a shiraz whose fruit is less assertive than many, making it more versatile with food. At the same time, it's well defined and layered, and it holds true right through the palate. It's dry, with easygoing tannins, and the acid–fruit balance is right on for food.

NOTES

....
....
....
....

★ ★ ★ ★ ½

Hardys 'Bankside' Shiraz 2012
SOUTH AUSTRALIA $14.65 (333948) **D**

[Vintages Essential] This is a shiraz that lies comfortably between the in-your-face, jammy shirazes and those that are restrained and highly structured. It delivers ripe and quite plush flavours with a core of fruit sweetness. It's dry with quite gripping tannins, and it has a full and generous texture that coats your mouth with flavour. Serve this with a rich meal, like lamb stew and sweet root vegetables.

NOTES

....
....

....

★ ★ ★ ★

Hardys 'Butcher's Gold' Shiraz/Sangiovese 2012

SOUTH AUSTRALIA $15.00 (219139) **XD**

Look for many more Australian wines made from Mediterranean varieties, like sangiovese, as plantings are expanding rapidly. Here the sangiovese brings high-toned fruit and acidity to the fruitiness of the shiraz, and the result is very attractive. The flavours have depth and complexity and the texture is fresh and juicy. This is a very good choice for red meats and for well-seasoned dishes in general.

NOTES

....

....

....

....

★ ★ ★ ★

Jacob's Creek Reserve Cabernet Sauvignon 2012

COONAWARRA $16.95   (91751) **XD**

Jacob's Creek wines are now firmly regional, and what better Australian region to draw cabernet from than Coonawarra? This is a lovely, ripe, cool-climate style in which the fruit is solid but not in your face and the acidity provides clean freshness. This is a wine you can enjoy glass after glass with all kinds of red meats. Try it with well-seasoned, braised short ribs.

NOTES

....

....

....

....

....

★ ★ ★ ★

Jacob's Creek Reserve Shiraz 2012

BAROSSA VALLEY $16.95 (665471) **XD**

Jacob's Creek is an actual creek that meanders through the Barossa wine region. It's undistinguished as bodies of water go, but the little winery on its bank that first produced wine in 1850 did earn distinction. This reserve shiraz is solid from start to finish, with flavours of ripe fruit paired with a rich, tangy texture. It goes well with grilled lamb.

NOTES

....

....

....

....

NEW!
★ ★ ★ ★ ★

Kilikanoon 'Killerman's Run' Shiraz 2011

AUSTRALIA $19.95 (925453) **D**

[Vintages Essential] This is one full-on shiraz, with the octane (14.5 percent alcohol) to power it. It's big bodied, with flavours that are intense and deep, yet broad and layered. And the acidity is well calibrated, too, as are the framing tannins. Wait! It's not just a fruit-bomb, but a well-made, structured wine that's a pleasure to drink with intensely flavoured red meats and seasoned sausages.

NOTES

....
....
....
....

★ ★ ★ ★

Lindemans 'Bin 99' Pinot Noir 2012

SOUTH EASTERN AUSTRALIA $11.95 (458661) **D**

Pinot noir made big strides in popularity in North America after it featured in the movie *Sideways*, but it isn't so big on the Australian wine scene. Even so, this is a pretty nice entry-level pinot that offers ripe fruit flavours. It's medium bodied and dry—a wine for all seasons and seasonings. Serve it on the patio with grilled lamb, pork or even poultry.

NOTES

....
....
....
....
....

★ ★ ★ ★

McGuigan 'Black Label' Shiraz 2012

SOUTH EASTERN AUSTRALIA $10.95 (325787) **D**

Delivering a lot for a little has made this a popular shiraz. It boasts plenty of concentrated fruit, with quite good complexity and a texture that's tangy and even vibrant, considering the density of the fruit. Dry and modestly tannic, it's a no-brainer for juicy burgers, barbecued ribs and well-seasoned red meats generally.

NOTES

....
....
....
....
....

McWilliam's 'Hanwood Estate' Shiraz 2012

★ ★ ★ ★

SOUTH EASTERN AUSTRALIA $14.95   (610683)   D

Many Australian shirazes in this price range taste very similar, so it's nice to come across one with some individuality. This has the layered ripe fruit flavours of a well-made shiraz, and some light oakiness from the barrels in which it was aged. Medium bodied and with a slightly tangy texture, it goes well with grilled lamb chops or a pepper steak.

NOTES
....
....
....
....
....

Mitolo 'Jester' Shiraz 2011

★ ★ ★ ★ ★

MCLAREN VALE $22.95   (659607)   D

[Vintages Essential] 'Jester' takes its name from Richard Tarlton, a favourite clown of Queen Elizabeth I, and it celebrates humour and intellect. It also celebrates quality wine and wonderful value. This is an impressive shiraz that speaks to style all the way through, from the well-structured and extracted flavours, through the rich and refreshing texture, to the fine balance. Drink it with full-flavoured red meats like well-seasoned lamb, pepper steak or a great burger.

NOTES
....
....
....

Mitolo 'Junior' Shiraz 2011

★ ★ ★ ★

MCLAREN VALE $16.95 (183947) XD

'Junior' is the younger sibling of Mitolo 'Jester' shiraz (see previous listing). A little less complex than 'Jester,' it nonetheless offers very good value. The flavours are concentrated and layered, the balance is right and a seam of fresh acidity carries everything along nicely. It goes well with red meats of all kinds, as well as hearty vegetarian risottos and paellas.

NOTES
....
....
....
....
....

Penfolds 'Koonunga Hill' Shiraz/Cabernet 2012

★ ★ ★ ★ ½

SOUTH AUSTRALIA $16.95 (285544) **XD**

Although the shiraz/cabernet sauvignon blend is also made elsewhere, Australia has made it its own, and this example shows the character well. Look for rich, ripe fruit that's sweet at the core and has layers of complexity and a tangy, fresh texture from the well-calibrated acidity. It's dry with moderate tannins and it's a great partner for grilled red meats.

NOTES

Penfolds 'Thomas Hyland' Shiraz 2012

★ ★ ★ ★ ½

ADELAIDE $21.95 (611210) **D**

[Vintages Essential] This big, luscious shiraz is named for the son-in-law of Dr. Penfold, who founded the company. Thomas would be delighted to be associated with it. It's an assertive red with intense fruit flavours and has a texture that's plush, dense and tangy. Between medium and full bodied, it's a sheer pleasure to drink—especially with well-seasoned red meat, like lamb with garlic and rosemary.

NOTES

Peter Lehmann 'Clancy's Legendary Red' 2011

★ ★ ★ ★ ½

BAROSSA VALLEY $17.95 (611467) **XD**

Clancy's is just about a household name in Australia, where it has won many awards. It's a delicious blend of shiraz, cabernet sauvignon and merlot, and it delivers terrific depth and breadth of flavour, enhanced by plenty of complexity. Full bodied with a dense, juicy texture, it's dry and carries its tannins lightly. It has a new label this year, but the quality's the same. You just can't go wrong pouring this with hearty red meat dishes.

NOTES

★ ★ ★ ★

Peter Lehmann 'Portrait' Shiraz 2012

BAROSSA VALLEY $19.95 (572875) **XD**

Peter Lehmann is one of the icons of the Australian wine industry, and his big, bold presence is reflected in some of his wines—like this one. It's a classic dry Barossa shiraz, with full, ripe fruit flavours, nice complexity and a stylish, tangy texture. It has high alcohol (14.5 percent), but it's well managed and balanced and it doesn't intrude into the flavours or texture. This is a perfect match for barbecued red meats.

NOTES

....

....

....

NEW!
★ ★ ★ ★ ½

Pirramimma 'Stock's Hill' GSM 2011

MCLAREN VALE $16.90 (352252) **D**

"GSM" stands for a blend of grenache, syrah/shiraz and mourvèdre/mataró. It originated in the Rhône Valley, but has been emulated in other regions. This iteration of the blend is richly and intensely flavoured, with impressive complexity and length. It's finely balanced, with a generous texture and supple tannins. It's a red meat wine.

NOTES

....

....

....

....

....

★ ★ ★ ★ ½

Red Knot Cabernet Sauvignon 2010

MCLAREN VALE $17.95 (91702) **XD**

It's not so much a knot on the label as an impossibly tangled piece of . . . string? The wine itself is a lot easier to unravel. First you get very pleasant and complex aromas (if you bother to sniff it), then a mouthful of lovely, rich fruit that's concentrated, focused and layered. The tannins are supple, the balance is right on. What's not to like? And it's even better with red meat or a hearty mushroom risotto.

NOTES

....

....

....

....

....

Red Knot Shiraz 2011

★ ★ ★ ★ ½

MCLAREN VALE $17.95 (619395) **D**

This wine has one of the more unusual closures. First you unwind the plastic tail (undo the knot, I suppose), then the whole thing comes off. After playing with that, you get to taste the wine, which is a bigger treat. It's plush and densely flavoured, with a generous and smooth texture. There's some tanginess there, too, and it's well balanced. This goes nicely with well-seasoned red meats like barbecued ribs.

NOTES

....
....
....
....

Ringbolt Cabernet Sauvignon 2011

★ ★ ★ ★ ½

MARGARET RIVER $19.95 (606624) **D**

[Vintages Essential] Margaret River is one of the wine regions of Western Australia, an area that has developed a reputation for high-quality wines. This cabernet is one of them. You'll find it has concentrated and full-on flavours, but that they're focused, complex and nicely balanced by the refreshing acidity. The tannins are ripe and supple. This is a great choice for grilled, roasted or braised red meats.

NOTES

....
....
....
....

Rosemount Estate 'Diamond Label' Shiraz 2012

★ ★ ★ ★ ½

SOUTH EASTERN AUSTRALIA $15.95 (302349) **D**

This is almost a classic Australian shiraz. It's been in the LCBO for many, many years, and the style has evolved nicely over time. It's all there: the rich, ripe flavours and the tangy texture that you expect. But it's not overbearing, not in your face. It's medium bodied with a dry, lightly tangy texture, has good structure and is excellent with grilled lamb chops or roasted lamb.

NOTES

....
....
....

Tempus Two Cabernet Merlot 2012

NEW!
★★★★

LIMESTONE COAST $16.90 (308197) **D**

The fruit go full-frontal here, with a generous serving of plush, ripe flavours that are well layered and consistent from start to finish. The texture is smooth and mouth filling, with good structure and supple tannins. The acidity is also well calibrated, contributing a freshness to everything. This is a good bet for many well-seasoned red meat dishes.

NOTES

....

....

....

....

....

Tic Tok Pocketwatch Cabernet Sauvignon 2011

NEW!
★★★★ ½

CENTRAL RANGES $15.95 (187179) **D**

From the Central Ranges wine region of New South Wales, this is an impressive cabernet that fits snugly into the reliable tic tok list. Look for concentrated and complex fruit here, sweet at the core and nicely layered. It's complemented by clean, fresh acidity, and framed by supple, manageable tannins. This is a great choice for many red meat dishes.

NOTES

....

....

....

....

....

Wolf Blass 'Red Label' Shiraz/Cabernet 2012

★★★★

SOUTH EASTERN AUSTRALIA $14.95 (311795) **XD**

The shiraz/cabernet blend was made famous by Australia, and this example shows why it's been so successful. It's rich in layers of flavour that sweep into your mouth on a tangy tide. The fruit is ripe and sweet, but this is dry and medium bodied, with light tannins. It's an excellent choice when you're serving grilled or roasted red meats or hearty stews.

NOTES

....

....

....

....

....

★ ★ ★ ★ **Wolf Blass 'Yellow Label' Cabernet Sauvignon 2012**

SOUTH AUSTRALIA $16.95 (251876) **XD**

There was a time when no self-respecting restaurant would leave this off its wine list. It was everyone's standby for steak and red meat in general—in fact, for any food. Taste it and you'll see the attraction. It's well made and delivers above par in flavour, texture and finish. You'll find fruit-packed flavours and a full, tangy texture in this dry, medium-bodied cab.

NOTES

....

....

....

....

....

★ ★ ★ ★ ½ **Wolf Blass 'Yellow Label' Shiraz 2012**

SOUTH AUSTRALIA $16.95 (506691) **XD**

This strays from the path that Australian shiraz has beaten for many years. The fruit intensity has been dialled back and the acidity dialled up a little, making for an excellent, food-friendly balance. Fruit concentration and complexity are there along with the classic flavour profile, so shiraz lovers won't suffer withdrawal symptoms. This is a very good choice for red meats and many hearty pasta dishes.

NOTES

....

....

....

....

★ ★ ★ ★ **Wyndham Estate 'Bin 444' Cabernet Sauvignon 2011**

SOUTH EASTERN AUSTRALIA $15.45 (110486) **XD**

Wyndham Estate does things right and achieves quality and value across the varietal board. This cabernet sauvignon presents flavours that have length, breadth and complexity, along with a texture that's rich, satisfying and refreshing. The tannins are present and manageable, especially when you drink this (as you might) with medium-rare beef or lamb, juicy burgers or an aged cheese such as cheddar or Parmigiano Reggiano.

NOTES

....

....

....

★ ★ ★ ★ ½ Wyndham Estate 'George Wyndham Founder's Reserve' Shiraz 2011

LANGHORNE CREEK $19.95 (107904) **XD**

Founded in 1828, Wyndham Estate is Australia's oldest operating winery. George Wyndham, an English immigrant, planted the country's first commercial shiraz vineyard. He had no idea what he'd started. This shiraz delivers plush and layered fruit flavours and a generous, smooth, mouth-filling texture that's also fresh and clean. It's a great choice for roasted or grilled lamb.

NOTES

....

....

....

★ ★ ★ ★ [yellow tail] Reserve Shiraz 2012

SOUTH EASTERN AUSTRALIA $15.95 (234609) **D**

Perhaps the subliminal attraction of [yellow tail] is the fact that the wallaby on the label has a gold and orange tail. Its thighs are yellow, but [yellow thigh] doesn't seem as effective as a brand. This is a plump and fruity shiraz with some complexity in the flavours and good acidity, making for a tangy texture. It's easy drinking and it goes well with grilled red meats and gourmet burgers.

NOTES

....

....

....

....

BRITISH COLUMBIA

BRITISH COLUMBIA'S WINERIES—most of which are located in the Okanagan Valley—produce many high-quality and well-priced red wines. Unfortunately, hardly any of it makes its way to Ontario.

The VQA (Vintners Quality Alliance) classification on British Columbia wine labels means that the grapes were grown in the region specified and that the wine has been tested and tasted by a panel.

★ ★ ★ ★

Mission Hill 'Five Vineyards' Cabernet/Merlot 2011

VQA OKAHAGAN VALLEY $16.45 (145102) **XD**

This well-made blend combines ripe fruit flavours with good acidity to make a red that goes with red meats, poultry, pork and many medium-flavoured cheeses. The fruit is ripe and well concentrated, with good layering and persistence. The acidity is fresh and juicy, and the tannins are drying but easygoing.

NOTES

....

....

....

....

★ ★ ★ ★ ½

Mission Hill Reserve Cabernet Sauvignon 2011

VQA OKANAGAN VALLEY $23.95 (553321) **D**

[Vintages Essential] Mission Hill helped put the Okanagan Valley wine region on the map, and the company's attention to detail has kept it in the forefront of British Columbia wine producers. This cabernet sauvignon is stylish and opulent. You'll find elegant fruit flavours and a rich, tangy texture. A bit more than medium bodied and dry, it goes nicely with well-seasoned red meats.

NOTES

....

....

....

....

....

★ ★ ★ ★ ★

Osoyoos Larose 'Le Grand Vin' 2009

VQA OKANAGAN VALLEY $44.95 (626325) **XD**

[Vintages Essential] Osoyoos Larose is one of Canada's iconic wines. Made from Bordeaux varieties, it delivers terrific complexity in the well-defined and focused flavours, fine fruit–acid balance and ripe, firm tannins. You can drink this now (with red meats—grilled lamb would be excellent) or cellar it through 2018 and beyond.

NOTES

....

....

....

....

....

BULGARIA

BULGARIA IS AN IMPORTANT wine-producing country that turns out some stunning reds, especially cabernet sauvignon and merlot. Unfortunately, few of them make their way to Canada, but there are some solid entry-level wines that represent good value.

Boyar Cabernet Sauvignon 2012

★ ★ ★ ★

REGIONAL WINE THRACIAN LOWLANDS $7.95   (340851) **D**

This is a very solid, mid-weight cabernet that goes well with roasted red meats, poultry, pork and many pasta dishes and pizzas. The fruit is ripe, the flavours are attractive, fresh and vibrant and the acidity is clean and refreshing. It's very dry (I'd have classed it x D), with quite drying but manageable tannins.

NOTES

....

....

....

....

CALIFORNIA

CALIFORNIA'S WINE INDUSTRY BEGAN in earnest in the 1850s soon after the Gold Rush subsided. The industry fell on hard times during Prohibition in the 1920s and early 1930s, but was given a boost when, in 1976, some California wines beat some of the best bordeaux in a blind tasting in Paris. California now accounts for 90 percent of the wine produced in the United States and is fourth in world production after France, Italy and Spain.

California's varied growing conditions are suitable for many different grape varieties and wine styles. The state's signature grape is zinfandel (the excuse for many zin-fully bad puns), but cabernet sauvignon is more important. Other significant varieties are merlot, shiraz/syrah and pinot noir.

Most of the value wines in this book are labelled "California," which means that producers can use grapes grown anywhere in the state. Important designated regions within the state include Napa Valley, Sonoma County and Paso Robles.

181 Merlot 2011

★ ★ ★ ★

LODI $16.95 (226530) **D**

This wine is named for the 181 clone of merlot, which is widely planted on the right bank of the Dordogne River in Bordeaux, the source of many prestigious merlots. The result here is quite elegant. It has all the fruit flavour and softness that you expect of merlot, but the texture has some sleekness and the tannins are fine and supple. Rather than pair this with red meat, try it with roast chicken or turkey.

NOTES

....

....

....

....

Aquinas Pinot Noir 2012

★ ★ ★ ★

NAPA VALLEY $18.95 (277657) **D**

This wine is actually named for St. Thomas Aquinas, for reasons outlined on the back label. The wine itself is less theological than stylish and compelling. It's fruit forward, but in a controlled way, with nice layered complexity, a smooth and fresh texture and light tannins. This is an easy choice for roast chicken and turkey, mushroom risotto and paella, and it stretches to simple red meat dishes, as well.

NOTES

....

....

....

....

Beringer 'California Collection' Cabernet Sauvignon 2011

★ ★ ★ ★

CALIFORNIA $9.95 (113001) **D**

This 'California Collection' cabernet sauvignon does what's intended: provides good quality at a very reasonable price. It's all solid fruit flavours that have good complexity and weight, and it has a texture that's satisfying and tangy. Dry and well balanced, it's a good choice for red meats, burgers and spicy sausages.

NOTES

....

....

....

....

....

★ ★ ★ ★ ½

Beringer 'Founder's Estate' Cabernet Sauvignon 2011

CALIFORNIA $17.95   (534263)   **D**

Beringer is the Napa Valley's oldest continuous wine producer, dating back to 1876. It stayed in business even during the dry days of Prohibition by making sacramental wine. This cabernet is delicious rather than spiritual, delivering a medium body, an intense and juicy texture and good solid fruit flavours. It's dry, the tannins are moderate and it goes very well with steak.

NOTES
....
....
....
....

★ ★ ★ ★

Beringer 'Founder's Estate' Zinfandel 2011

CALIFORNIA $17.95   (308205)   **D**

There's plenty of concentrated fruit in this zinfandel, as you would expect, but it's not as overbearing as many zins. You'll find it well pitched, with a good level of complexity, and in good balance with the acidity. It's dry, with slightly grippy tannins. This is a very good choice for red meats, winter stews, gourmet burgers and hearty tomato-based pasta dishes.

NOTES
....
....
....
....

★ ★ ★ ★ ★

Beringer 'Knights Valley' Cabernet Sauvignon 2011

KNIGHTS VALLEY $37.95   (352583)   **D**

[Vintages Essential] This is a stunning wine, vintage after vintage. It achieves the feat that distinguishes many fine wines of being both bold and stylish at the same time. The flavours are deep, broad and intricately layered, the texture is plump, plush and generous, and the acidity is beautifully handled. The tannins are still gripping, so you might decant it for two or three hours to enjoy with beef grilled or roasted no more than medium rare.

NOTES
....
....
....
....

★ ★ ★ ★

Big House Cardinal Zin 2012

CALIFORNIA $12.95 (272401) D

For some reason, zinfandel attracts bad puns, but the creator of this wine (and Big House Red, next) delights in them even more. You can groan, but you'll like the wines. This zinfandel, made from old vines, is full of zin flavour that's concentrated and layered from start to finish. It's dry with good acidity, and it goes well with ribs, burgers and grilled red meats.

NOTES

....

....

....

....

....

★ ★ ★ ★ ½

Big House Red 2012

CALIFORNIA $12.95 (178632) D

This blend of weird grape varieties has intrigued wine lovers for years. But in the end, it's just very good wine and value. Look for concentrated, ripe, layered flavours, acidity that's very well balanced and easygoing tannins. This is a terrific barbecue wine (think burgers, ribs and sausages), but it performs just as well indoors with all kinds of red meats.

NOTES

....

....

....

....

★ ★ ★ ★ ½

Bonterra Cabernet Sauvignon 2011

MENDOCINO COUNTY/LAKE COUNTY $19.95 (342428) D

[Vintages Essential] This is an organic wine, meaning that the grapes were grown without the use of chemical fertilizers or herbicides. This cabernet sauvignon includes a little merlot, syrah and other red varieties, and they add up to a delicious red with a full but sleek texture from the acidity. The flavours are focused and layered. This is a great cabernet for red meats and hearty stews.

NOTES

....

....

....

....

....

Buena Vista Pinot Noir 2011

★ ★ ★ ★ ½

CARNEROS $25.05 (304105) **XD**

This is a very attractive pinot noir from one of California's premium pinot regions. Look for well-focused ripe-sweet flavours right through the palate, with fresh acidity contributing a tangy, almost juicy texture. The tannins are moderate and drying. This is a great choice for many dishes, especially grilled lamb, roast turkey and grilled salmon.

NOTES

....

....

....

....

....

Chateau St. Jean Pinot Noir 2012

★ ★ ★ ★ ★

CALIFORNIA $19.95 (308221) **D**

This is a lovely pinot noir, definitely in a west coast style, with solid fruit that's well focused, nicely complex and structured. The acidity shines through and gives the wine some fresh juiciness, and the tannins are ripe and present yet understated. It's an excellent choice for roast turkey and chicken, roast and grilled pork and grilled seasoned sausages.

NOTES

....

....

....

....

....

Cline Zinfandel 2012

★ ★ ★ ★

LODI $14.15 (489278) **D**

This is a good example of a zinfandel made to go with food. Unlike too many high-octane, high-performance zins that leave food in the dust, this one has a refreshing texture (not a heavy, low-acid one), and the concentrated ripe flavours are layered. It's medium bodied and the very dry texture works well with its fruitiness. It's a natural for juicy hamburgers or other well-seasoned red meats.

NOTES

....

....

....

....

Clos du Bois Cabernet Sauvignon 2011

★ ★ ★ ★ ½

NORTH COAST $15.95 (308304) **XD**

This is a big-bodied, fruit-forward cabernet that's dry and full of ripe fruit flavour from start to finish. It's nicely balanced, with a broad seam of clean acidity holding the weight of the fruit in check, with easygoing tannins and a tangy texture. It's a natural for red meats and, at the barbecue, for burgers and sausages.

NOTES

....

....

....

....

Dancing Bull 'Vintage Blend' Zinfandel 2011

★ ★ ★ ★

CALIFORNIA $13.95   (669499) **D**

The dancing bull occupies a small part of the label, making this look less like a "critter wine." But he still looks pretty happy and he's choreographed a zin that stresses ripe fruit flavours over sheer power. The texture is substantial and plush, but it manages to be fresh and light on its feet . . . or hoofs. This is a zin you can happily pair with ribs or a steak with barbecue sauce.

NOTES

....

....

....

De Loach 'Heritage Reserve' Pinot Noir 2011

★ ★ ★ ★ ½

CALIFORNIA $15.95 (220434) **XD**

This is a very attractive pinot noir in a fruit-forward, California style. Look for fruit that's rich and full, with plenty of layered complexity. The acidity comes through very effectively, taming the fruit richness and adding some freshness to the texture. With soft, supple tannins, this is a good bet for grilled red meats and rich mushroom dishes.

NOTES

....

....

....

....

★ ★ ★ ★

Dreaming Tree 'Crush' Red 2011

CALIFORNIA $16.95   (310391)   **D**

Mostly merlot and zinfandel, this is an easy-drinking red blend that offers plenty of ripe-sweet fruit and good fruit–acid balance. It's dry, but there's a little sweetness in the flavours, and as an added bonus you get decent complexity and good structure. This is a red wine you can drink on its own, but you can also easily pair it with well-seasoned red meats, burgers and spicy sausages.

NOTES

....
....
....
....

★ ★ ★ ★

Fetzer 'Valley Oaks' Cabernet Sauvignon 2011

CALIFORNIA $13.95   (336974)   **D**

This is a very good mid-range, dry, medium-bodied cabernet (with 2 percent petite sirah) that's simply well made and very attractive. It goes well with the usual cabernet suspects—red meats, burgers, grilled sausages—but it extends to roast pork and poultry. There's nothing paltry about the wine itself, which shows slightly floral aromas, concentrated flavours, good complexity and structure, and a fresh, tangy texture.

NOTES

....
....
....
....

★ ★ ★ ★ ½

Firestone Cabernet Sauvignon 2011

SANTA YNEZ VALLEY $19.90 (292128)   **XD**

This delicious cabernet shows concentrated, ripe, layered and structured fruit right through the palate, and out the other side. It has a spine of clean, fresh acidity that comes through almost as juiciness, and the tannins are firm but manageable. It's an obvious candidate for red meats, such as grilled steak, game and lamb.

NOTES

....
....
....
....

Gnarly Head 'Cab' Cabernet Sauvignon 2011

★ ★ ★ ★

CALIFORNIA $15.05 (68924) **D**

The label shows a stylized and very gnarly grapevine, making you think this could be from old vines. There's no such claim, but the wine has the concentrated flavour you often expect from more mature vines. Look for intense, sweet fruit flavours here, with a generous texture and drying tannins. It's medium-to-full in weight and goes with heavier dishes, like steak.

NOTES
....
....
....
....

Hahn Pinot Noir 2012

★ ★ ★ ★

MONTEREY COUNTY $18.95 (226555) **D**

This is distinctly in the style known as "New World," with the fruit up front—and fruit that's ripe (with a sweet core), complex and persistent right through the palate. It's paired with the fresh acidity that's the hallmark of successful pinot noir, and shows easygoing tannins. Ready to drink now, this goes well with roast lamb, pork and poultry, as well as grilled salmon and hearty vegetarian dishes, like a mushroom risotto.

NOTES
....
....
....
....

J. Lohr 'Seven Oaks' Cabernet Sauvignon 2011

★ ★ ★ ★ ½

PASO ROBLES $21.95 (656561) **XD**

[Vintages Essential] Paso Robles is a region that has quickly earned a reputation for high-quality wines. This well-balanced cabernet sauvignon shows lovely, ripe fruit flavours that are well defined and layered and accompanied by a seam of fresh acidity that contributes an attractive tangy texture. The tannins are easygoing, and this is a great choice for grilled or roasted red meats.

NOTES
....
....
....
....

NEW!
★ ★ ★ ★

Kenwood Zinfandel 2010

SONOMA COUNTY $20.50 (350462) **D**

This is a fairly opulent zinfandel that really delivers on the fruit; look for generous and plush flavours with real depth, structure and complexity. The texture is full and smooth, and the acidity comes through to rein in the fruitiness. With modest tannins, it's a very good choice for well-seasoned red meats and many barbecued foods.

NOTES

....

....

....

....

....

★ ★ ★ ★ ★

Liberty School Cabernet Sauvignon 2011

PASO ROBLES $19.95 (738823) **D**

[Vintages Essential] This is one of the great buys in the LCBO at this price point; it over-delivers on everything and shouts its California pedigree. Look for compelling, concentrated, rich and ripe flavours with layered complexity; a generous, mouth-filling, tangy texture; sweet, drying tannins; and a finish that stays with you. It's a natural for rich red meat dishes.

NOTES

....

....

....

....

NEW!
★ ★ ★ ★ ★

Liberty School Zinfandel 2010

PASO ROBLES $18.95   (41095) **D**

[Vintages Essential] This is a delicious zinfandel that shows all the intensity and depth of fruit you expect from the variety. The fruit is ripe and sweet, but it's reined in by a good dose of acidity that lightens the wine. With nice layering and good structure, this wine goes well with well-seasoned grilled red meats, gourmet burgers and spicy barbecued sausages.

NOTES

....

....

....

....

★ ★ ★ ★

Louis M. Martini Cabernet Sauvignon 2010

SONOMA COUNTY $18.95 (292151) **D**

The name 'Martini' might not seem that promising for a winery—can you imagine James Bond asking for "a Martini cab, shaken not stirred"?—but the results are what's important. This is a lovely cabernet, with concentrated and well-defined flavours that are consistent from start to long finish. It's well balanced, with supple, easily approached tannins, and it goes well with all manner of red meats and other hearty dishes.

NOTES

....

....

....

....

★ ★ ★ ★

Ménage à Trois Red 2012

CALIFORNIA $16.95 (308007) **D**

Made from zinfandel, merlot and cabernet sauvignon, you'd expect this to be a big-boned wine, and it is. The flavours are broad and deep, solid right through and nicely complex. The tannins are drying and the acidity holds the weight of the fruit in check. This is a red for sharing with your two best friends as you down grilled red meat.

NOTES

....

....

....

....

....

NEW!
★ ★ ★ ★

Mirassou Pinot Noir 2012

CALIFORNIA $13.95 (185249) **D**

This is a light to medium–bodied and easy-drinking pinot noir that goes well with poultry, pork and grilled salmon, as well as with many tomato-based pasta dishes. The flavours are fruity and bright, well-focused and nicely concentrated. The acidity is clean and refreshing and the tannins are easygoing.

NOTES

....

....

....

....

....

Ravenswood 'Old Vines Vintners Blend' Zinfandel 2012

★ ★ ★ ★ ½

CALIFORNIA $17.95 (359257) **XD**

[Vintages Essential] If there's such a thing as a classic California zinfandel, this wine, with its plush, ripe fruit flavours, might be it. But it's also dry and moderately tannic, and it has an elegance you don't always find in high-octane zinfandels. This one is full flavoured, to be sure, but it's light on its feet and has a clean, fresh texture that makes it especially good for food. Open this, summer or winter, when you're serving grilled red meats.

NOTES

....

....

....

....

Raymond 'Family Classic' Cabernet Sauvignon 2012

★ ★ ★ ★ ½

NORTH COAST $18.95 (269761) **D**

The North Coast appellation is a vast area that includes most of California's wineries. This cabernet is full of fruit and the flavours are solid from start to finish. It's dry and lightly tannic, lies between medium and full bodied and shows a fairly plush but refreshing texture. It's built for well-flavoured food, so try it with seasoned red meats and stews.

NOTES

....

....

....

....

Robert Mondavi Cabernet Sauvignon 2010

★ ★ ★ ★ ★

NAPA VALLEY $34.95 (255513) **D**

[Vintages Essential] How much should you pay for a Napa cab? Only the fare shown on the meter. The tariff here is a bit more than you usually find in the LCBO, but—wow!—this is a delicious cabernet. It's elegant and stylish right through, with luscious and complex flavours. It's dry and medium bodied, with moderate tannins and a sleek and quite refreshing texture. Serve it with rack of lamb or other grilled red meat.

NOTES

....

....

....

....

★ ★ ★ ★   **Robert Mondavi 'Private Selection'**
Cabernet Sauvignon 2012

CENTRAL COAST $17.95   (392225)   **D**

The 'Private Selection' series is known for quality and value, and this cabernet sauvignon fits in seamlessly. The flavours are well extracted and nicely layered, the texture is generous and smooth but refreshing, and the tannins are firm and manageable. This is a natural for roasted or grilled red meats, but it extends to rich pasta dishes and aged cheeses such as cheddar.

NOTES

....

....

....

....

★ ★ ★ ★   **Robert Mondavi 'Private Selection' Pinot Noir 2012**

CALIFORNIA $17.95   (465435)   **D**

This pinot noir is a real pleasure to drink, and it lives up to the quality that the Mondavi name is associated with. You'll find it has quite intense and vibrant flavours of fresh, ripe fruit, with a smooth, easy-drinking texture and light tannins. Dry and medium bodied, it's a fine choice for grilled planked salmon or for roast turkey or chicken with cranberries.

NOTES

....

....

....

....

★ ★ ★ ★ ½   **Rodney Strong Pinot Noir 2011**

RUSSIAN RIVER VALLEY $24.95 (954834)   **D**

[Vintages Essential] Russian River Valley is a cool area of California that's earned a reputation for fine pinot noirs. This is a very good example, with beautifully focused fruit that's layered and consistent right through the palate. It's supported by bright acidity and framed by supple tannins. Everything is in order for grilled lamb, duck breast or roasted red meats.

NOTES

....

....

....

....

....

Sledgehammer Zinfandel 2011

★ ★ ★ ★

NORTH COAST $17.95 (230466) **D**

The Sledgehammer brand was designed for men: a bold design, macho name and big wines (no rosé in the range, of course!). But you don't need to be brawny and inarticulate to enjoy the wines. This zinfandel is big, as zins tend to be, but it has complexity, structure and good balance. Still, better to pair it with a manly meal like steak or other red meat.

NOTES

....

....

....

....

....

Smoking Loon Cabernet Sauvignon 2012

★ ★ ★ ★

CALIFORNIA $14.95   (55517) **D**

Why is this loon smoking? Because this is a smokin' cabernet? It's chock full of rich, sweet fruit flavours, and it has an attractive texture that's quite mouth filling but still refreshing and good with food. The tannins are drying and manageable. Drink this with grilled red meats at the cottage while you're listening for the loons to call. Can't hear them? It's because they've taken up smoking and can't call with cigars in their beaks.

NOTES

....

....

....

....

Stags' Leap Cabernet Sauvignon 2011

★ ★ ★ ★ ★

NAPA VALLEY $49.95 (996405) **XD**

[Vintages Essential] This is a lovely cabernet that shows why the variety became so closely identified with the region that "Napa cab" seems a natural pairing. You can also pair this with red meats to take advantage of its good weight and texture and the ripe, moderate tannins. The flavours are concentrated and layered and show considerable depth, and they're harnessed to fresh, food-friendly acidity.

NOTES

....

....

....

....

NEW!
★ ★ ★ ★ ½

Sterling Napa Valley Cabernet Sauvignon 2011

NAPA VALLEY $29.95 (314575) **D**

[Vintages Essential] Another Napa cabernet, this one characterized by intense flavours that are solid right through the palate and out the other side. Look for good layering and structure, medium-plus body, and a smooth texture, with easygoing tannins. It's almost a textbook cabernet. Drink it with roasted or grilled red meats, savoury sausages and gourmet beef- or game-burgers.

NOTES

....

....

....

....

NEW!
★ ★ ★ ★ ½

Sterling Napa Valley Merlot 2011

NAPA VALLEY $27.95 (330241) **XD**

[Vintages Essential] Napa merlot is too often overshadowed by better-known cabernet sauvignon (the "Napa cab" thing), but the region turns out excellent merlots, too. This one is characterized by concentrated, generous and well-defined fruit, with very good complexity and structure. The acidity clicks in, fresh and clean, and the tannins are ripe, supple and drying. It's an excellent choice for grilled lamb and other red meats.

NOTES

....

....

....

....

NEW!
★ ★ ★ ★

Sterling 'Vintner's Collection' Cabernet Sauvignon 2011

CENTRAL COAST $15.95 (56366)   **D**

This is a fine medium-to-full-bodied cabernet that delivers rich and luscious fruit all through the palate. For all the weight in the fruit, it's relatively easy drinking because of the well-calibrated acidity, and to that we must add good structure and complexity. It's an easy choice for grilled or roasted red meats (including burgers) and for hearty winter stews.

NOTES

....

....

....

....

....

Wente 'Southern Hills' Cabernet Sauvignon 2011

★ ★ ★ ★ ½

LIVERMORE VALLEY/SAN FRANCISCO BAY $16.95 (301507)   D

These regions near San Francisco were first planted with vines by Spanish missionaries in the 1760s. The Wente family arrived a little later, in the 1840s. Powerful, intense and full of layers of rich fruit flavour, this full-bodied cabernet delivers a texture that's mouth filling and refreshing. The tannins are firm but manageable. This is a great choice when you're eating red meat grilled or roasted no more than medium rare.

NOTES

Woodbridge Cabernet Sauvignon 2012

★ ★ ★ ★

CALIFORNIA $12.95   (48611)   D

Woodbridge is a Robert Mondavi brand that's designed to give good quality at a good price—good value, in other words. And this cabernet does, with solid fruit flavours and nice balance. It's medium bodied and dry, has a soft, low-tannin texture and goes very well with burgers and grilled red meats.

NOTES

NEW!
★ ★ ★ ★

Zinfatuation Zinfandel 2012

AMADOR COUNTY $16.95   (274746)   D

Zintroducing another wordplay on zinfandel, the variety that has given us an apparently zinfinite number of "zin" phrases like "zinfully delicious" and "seven deadly zins." This is a well-made zin that shows classic depth, intensity, and ripeness in the flavours, along with good structure, fruit–acid balance and smooth texture. Enjoy it with grilled, well-seasoned red meats and sausages.

NOTES

CHILE

CHILE PRODUCES MANY OF THE BEST-VALUE red wines in the LCBO. They tend to be bold and full of flavour, including carmenère (Chile's signature variety), cabernet sauvignon, merlot, shiraz/syrah and pinot noir, as well as blends.

What makes Chile such a good source for quality red wine? Climate and location are the keys. Most Chilean wine regions are in warm, sun-soaked valleys. Maipo and Colchagua are two, and they're both well represented among the wines here. As Chile's wines gain the following they deserve and sales increase, expect prices to do the same. In the meantime, enjoy Chile's reds for their great quality and value at lower prices.

Designated Chilean wine regions are indicated after the letters DO (*Denominación de Origen*).

★ ★ ★ ★

35° South Reserva Cabernet Sauvignon 2012

DO CENTRAL VALLEY $12.95   (170019)   **D**

This cabernet is full of ripe fruit. The flavours are concentrated and quite dense, but they're offset by fresh acidity that reins the fruit in, and framed by ripe, somewhat drying tannins. There's some juiciness from the acidity that tilts the wine toward the table, and it's a good bet for many red meat dishes, whether cooked on the barbecue or prepared as a hearty stew.

NOTES

....

....

....

....

....

★ ★ ★ ★

Caliterra Reserva Cabernet Sauvignon 2012

DO COLCHAGUA VALLEY $9.95   (257329) **XD**

This is a basic, uncomplicated cabernet sauvignon that presents solid fruit flavours with moderate complexity and good fruit–acid balance. It's quite dry, with negligible tannins, and has a tangy texture. It's a good choice for burgers and barbecued ribs, and generally for any red meat from the grill.

NOTES

....

....

....

....

....

★ ★ ★ ★ ★

Carmen Gran Reserva Cabernet Sauvignon 2011

DO MAIPO ALTO $16.95   (358309) **XD**

Maipo Alto is a sub-region of the Maipo Valley, now recognized as one of the best areas, if not the best area, in Chile for cabernet sauvignon. It's cooled by the Andean winds and the cabernets are as fresh as they can be powerful. This example shows impressive complexity, with concentrated and defined fruit and a sleek texture framed by supple tannins. It's a natural for well-seasoned red meats.

NOTES

....

....

....

....

....

Carmen Reserva Carmenère 2012

★ ★ ★ ★

DO COLCHAGUA VALLEY $11.45 (169052) **XD**

In Chile, carmenère was long thought to be a variant of merlot until it was identified, in 1994, in one of the vineyards of the Carmen winery, which makes this wine. (There's no relationship between Carmen and carmenère.) This example is full of concentrated fruit and shows good balance and some complexity. It's plush and fruity and it goes well with red meats and grilled spicy sausages.

NOTES

Casillero del Diablo Reserva Cabernet Sauvignon 2012

★ ★ ★ ★

DO CENTRAL VALLEY $13.95 (278416) **XD**

Concha y Toro, one of Chile's major wine producers, came up with a winner in this Casillero del Diablo range, which offers very good value across the board. The cabernet sauvignon delivers a solid flavour profile, with quite good complexity and a nice tanginess in the texture. It's dry, with light to medium tannins, and a natural for grilled red meats.

NOTES

Casillero del Diablo Reserva Carmenère 2012

★ ★ ★ ★ ½

DO RAPEL VALLEY $13.95 (620666) **XD**

Is it a coincidence that a wine named for "the devil's cellar" was given a product code that included the numbers 666? And what was it the devil called when he tried to lure a victim into his cellar? "Carmenère!" This example of Chile's iconic grape is full of fruit power but is well defined and textured. It's medium to full in body and has an edgy tanginess that invites food. Send in a piece of grilled red meat.

NOTES

Casillero del Diablo Reserva Shiraz 2012

★ ★ ★ ★

DO RAPEL VALLEY $13.95 (568055) **XD**

This range of wines is named for a cellar at the Concha y Toro winery. The story goes that in order to deter workers from going into the cellar to drink wine, the owner told them it was inhabited by the devil. Too bad for them if they missed out on the likes of this. It's an intensely flavoured, well-balanced, dry, tangy-textured, lightly tannic red, and it goes well with barbecued red meats.

NOTES

Concha y Toro 'Marques de Casa Concha' Cabernet Sauvignon 2012

★ ★ ★ ★ ★

DO PUENTE ALTO $21.95 (337238) **XD**

[Vintages Essential] Concha y Toro produces huge volumes of quality wine, but this is one of their limited-production brands. The grapes come from a single vineyard (always considered a plus), and the wine is oak-aged for 14 months. What you get for a very good price is an elegant, well-structured red with layers of flavours and a superlative texture. Serve it with a good cut of red meat, cooked no more than medium rare.

NOTES

Concha y Toro 'Xplorador' Carmenère 2011

★ ★ ★ ★

DO CENTRAL VALLEY $10.95 (177816) **D**

It's not a very complicated carmenère, but it captures the rich fruitiness of the variety and harnesses it to the acidity that translates into attractive juiciness. It's fruit forward and medium bodied, and you can't go wrong serving this with burgers, barbecued ribs and grilled red meats.

NOTES

Cono Sur 'Bicicleta' Pinot Noir 2013

★ ★ ★ ★ ½

DO CENTRAL VALLEY $10.95   (341602)   **D**

Cono Sur is by far Chile's biggest producer of pinot noir. This one has the intense flavour you expect from a Chilean wine, but it's subtle enough to capture the classic textures and character of the variety. Look for concentrated flavours and a lively, food-friendly texture. Dry and medium bodied, it has light tannins and goes very well with grilled salmon or lamb.

NOTES

Cono Sur 'Bicicleta' Shiraz 2012

★ ★ ★ ★

DO COLCHAGUA VALLEY $9.95   (64295)   **XD**

This is a shiraz-dominant blend, with malbec, carmenère and cabernet sauvignon playing minor roles. The result is a medium-bodied, dry red with rich flavours that are dense and (for this price) remarkably complex. It has moderate tannins and a juicy texture. This is a very good buy and a great choice for grilled red meats, burgers and hearty vegetarian stews.

NOTES

Errazuriz 'Estate Series' Carmenère 2012

NEW!
★ ★ ★ ★

DO RAPEL VALLEY $13.95   (16238)   **D**

Errazuriz recently opened one of the most impressive wineries in Chile, and the fruit for this wine comes from the surrounding vineyards. You'll find plenty of ripe-sweet fruit in this bottle. It's solid from start to finish, shows nice layering, and it's supported by clean, refreshing acidity. The tannins are easygoing. Pair it with grilled or roasted red meats.

NOTES

Errazuriz 'Max Reserva' Cabernet Sauvignon 2011

★ ★ ★ ★

DO ACONCAGUA VALLEY $18.95 (335174) **XD**

This is a fruit-forward cabernet with concentrated, well-layered and persistent flavours from start to finish. It's well structured and the fruit–acid balance is good, with the acidity complementing the weight of the fruit effectively. The tannins are easygoing. Enjoy this cabernet with barbecued red meats and well-seasoned sausages.

NOTES

....

....

....

....

....

Errazuriz 'Max Reserva' Syrah 2011

★ ★ ★ ★ ★

DO ACONCAGUA VALLEY $18.95 (614750) **XD**

This is a very attractive, full-bodied syrah that delivers layered and concentrated flavours that are consistent right through the palate and hang on afterward. It's well structured, and the fruit is balanced by good acidity that translates to a tangy, almost juicy texture. It's a natural for red meats, hearty stews and pastas and many gourmet burgers.

NOTES

....

....

....

....

....

Lapostolle Casa 'Gran Selección' Carmenère 2012

NEW!
★ ★ ★ ★ ★

DO RAPEL VALLEY $16.05 (168740) **XD**

This is a very fine carmenère that packages the concentrated fruit flavour expected from the variety in a stylish form. The fruit is ripe, sleek and layered, and the acidity is fresh and appropriate, while the texture is sleek and juicy and inviting to food. The tannins are present and manageable. It's drinking beautifully, and goes well with grilled and roasted red meats.

NOTES

....

....

....

....

....

★ ★ ★ ★ ½ **Montes 'Limited Selection'**
Cabernet Sauvignon/Carmenère 2011

DO COLCHAGUA VALLEY $14.90 (292169) **XD**

This delicious full-bodied blend is 70 percent cabernet and 30 percent carmenère. With the fruit forward, it shows rich, plush flavours with breadth and complex depth, good structure, drying tannins and plenty of freshness in the texture. Everything holds together very well, and it's a great choice for grilled red meats.

NOTES

....

....

....

....

★ ★ ★ ★ ½ **Montes Reserva Cabernet Sauvignon 2012**

DO COLCHAGUA VALLEY $13.50 (157883) **D**

In one of the barrel rooms at the Montes winery, the barrels are serenaded by Gregorian chants, 24/7. Maybe you can pick up the echoes here. If not, you'll still be happy with the intense flavours, complexity and depth of the fruit, the moderately-gripping tannins and the excellent fruit–acid balance. This is a terrific choice for steak and other grilled red meats, as well as stronger cheeses.

NOTES

....

....

....

....

★ ★ ★ ★ ½ **MontGras Reserva Cabernet Sauvignon 2012**

DO COLCHAGUA VALLEY $11.90 (619205) **D**

This is an impressive cabernet, full of rich, plush, concentrated fruit that's layered and that shows good structure. It's full bodied and dry, with moderate tannins, and it has a texture that manages to be plump and mouth filling yet fresh at the same time. Think of this when you're serving well-seasoned grilled or roasted red meats.

NOTES

....

....

....

....

★ ★ ★ ★ ★
Pérez Cruz Reserva Cabernet Sauvignon 2012
DO MAIPO ALTO VALLEY $15.95 (694208) **D**

[Vintages Essential] Vintage after vintage, this opulent cabernet sauvignon, from Chile's key cabernet region, is full of delicious layered flavours. You can smell the rich aromas as you pour the wine into your glass. The texture is full, smooth and generous. For all its complexity, this is a dry wine with moderate tannins. It's perfect with well-seasoned red meat, like lamb with garlic and rosemary.

NOTES

NEW!
★ ★ ★ ★
Root: 1 Carmenère 2012
DO COLCHAGUA VALLEY $12.80 (350546)

This is a full-bodied carmenère with upfront flavours that are consistent from start to finish. The fruit is plush and generous with good complexity and structure, and it is supported by enough acidity to suit the wine for food. This is a very good wine for barbecued red meats, as well as for burgers and ribs.

NOTES

★ ★ ★ ★
Santa Carolina Reserva Cabernet Sauvignon 2011
DO COLCHAGUA VALLEY $12.95 (275925) **XD**

This is a gutsy cabernet, full of fruit that's dense and layered and shot through with a seam of acidity that lightens and freshens the texture. The balance is good—it's light on its feet for fruit this weighty—and the tannins are drying. You'll want food with heft for this cabernet, so think of well-seasoned lamb or a pepper steak.

NOTES

Santa Digna Reserve Cabernet Sauvignon 2012

★ ★ ★ ★ ½

DO CENTRAL VALLEY $14.95 (323881) **D**

From Chile's big Central Valley region, this 100 percent cabernet delivers rich, plush and layered flavours, complemented and reined in by acidity that translates as a tangy texture. Dry, with moderate and supple tannins, it goes well with seasoned red meat, like a New York strip loin and a shake or two of steak spice. It's a certified fair trade wine.

NOTES

....

....

....

....

Santa Rita Reserva Cabernet Sauvignon 2011

★ ★ ★ ★

DO MAIPO VALLEY $13.95 (253872) **XD**

Santa Rita has one of the most beautiful estates in Chile, and you get only a hint of it from the sketch on the bottle's label. What's more important is the wine inside. This is a very attractive cabernet sauvignon from one of Chile's premium cabernet regions. With quite intense flavours and a texture that's complex, layered and tangy, this dry and medium-bodied red is a very good choice for grilled or roasted red meats.

NOTES

....

....

....

....

Santa Rita Reserva Carmenère 2011

★ ★ ★ ★

DO RAPEL VALLEY $13.95 (177774) **XD**

As you would expect from carmenère, this shows concentrated fruit flavours. But it's no mindless fruit-bomb; the ripe and sweet fruit is nicely calibrated, with some complexity, and it's well balanced with the acidity. Lightly tannic, this is a red that goes well with well-seasoned red meats. It's a popular summer choice for barbecues and in winter it's a natural for hearty stews.

NOTES

....

....

....

....

....

Volcanes 'Summit Reserva'
Cabernet Sauvignon/Syrah 2012

DO RAPEL VALLEY $10.95 (350553) **XD**

This delivers plenty of solid flavours that include some spiciness from the syrah. (Try the two side-by-side to appreciate the different blends.) The fruit is nicely balanced by bright and tangy acidity, and this dry, medium-bodied red is versatile at the table. Drink it with red meats, poultry and pork and with seasoned sausages.

NOTES
....
....
....

FRANCE

FRANCE IS THE WORLD'S LARGEST and one of the most important wine producers, and has scores of wines in the LCBO. For many years, French wine was widely believed to be the best in the world, and bordeaux and burgundies were held up as the only wines worth drinking if you wanted to taste excellence. That's no longer so, as wine lovers have discovered the great wines made elsewhere. However, France continues to make high-quality and value-priced wine, as this list shows.

French wine labels display a few terms worth knowing. Wines labelled *Appellation d'Origine Contrôlée* (abbreviated AOC in this book) or *Appellation d'Origine Protégée* (AOP) have the highest-quality classification in France. They're made under tight rules that regulate aspects like the grape varieties that can be used in each region.

Wines labelled *Vin de Pays* or IGP (*Indication Géographique Protégée*) are regional wines made with fewer restrictions. They must be good quality, but producers have much more flexibility in the grapes they can use and how much wine they can make. *Vins de Pays d'Oc* (the ancient region of Occitanie) are by far the most important of the *Vins de Pays* wines.

★ ★ ★ ★

Albert Bichot 'Vieilles Vignes' Bourgogne Pinot Noir 2012

AOC BOURGOGNE $15.95 (166959) XD

'Vieilles Vignes' refers to "old vines." There's no standard definition of "old" in any wine law, but as vines age, they produce fewer but more intensely flavoured grapes, so producers like to highlight them. The flavours in this pinot are well concentrated and quite complex, and they're complemented by juicy acidity. Dry and lightly tannic, it's a very good choice for mushroom risotto, duck, lamb and roast turkey.

NOTES

....

....

....

....

★ ★ ★ ★ ½

Antonin Rodet Côtes du Rhône 2010

AOC CÔTES DU RHÔNE $14.00   (8979) XD

Antonin Rodet started making wine in Burgundy in 1875, and the winery now produces wines under various labels in many other French regions. This côtes du Rhône has a very attractive texture: juicy and generous and ideal for food. The flavours have good depth, and the wine is dry and medium bodied, pitched just right for your meal, especially veal or lamb, but turkey or chicken, too.

NOTES

....

....

....

....

NEW!
★ ★ ★ ★ ½

Bouchard Père & Fils Beaune du Château Premier Cru 2009

AOC BEAUNE PREMIER CRU $36.90 (325142) XD

This is a serious and seriously enjoyable pinot noir that delivers plenty of complexity and style. The flavours are many-layered, and they're consistent right through the palate. The spine of acidity is balanced, and the wine is dry to the point of astringency, a texture that carries through to the finish. The tannins are drying and manageable. Drink it with duck and rich poultry dishes (like coq au vin).

NOTES

....

....

....

Bouchard Père & Fils 'La Vignée' Pinot Noir 2011

★ ★ ★ ★

AOC BOURGOGNE $17.95 (605667) XD

If you're looking for a stylish red to go with turkey and cranberries, roast chicken, baked ham or summer salads, this pinot noir is an excellent candidate. It's made in the understated style often found in Burgundy. Don't be put off by the light colour; the flavours are nicely concentrated, with quite good complexity. It's dry, with moderate and manageable tannins, and well structured.

NOTES
....
....
....
....

Château de Courteillac 2012

★ ★ ★ ★ ½

AOC BORDEAUX $12.45 (360552) XD

This is a merlot-dominant blend, with contributions from cabernet sauvignon and cabernet franc. It's a solid, well-made red with concentrated flavours, some complexity and very good balance. Medium bodied and dry with light tannins, it's very versatile with food, and it goes well with many red meat, poultry and pork dishes.

NOTES
....
....
....
....
....

Château de Gourgazaud 2011

★ ★ ★ ★

AOC MINERVOIS $12.95 (22384) XD

This is one of the LCBO's veterans, and it earns its longevity not through inertia but by delivering quality and value, vintage after vintage. The aromas and flavours are fairly intense and complex, and the texture is rich, mouth filling and slightly tangy. Add medium weight, good balance and drying tannins and you have a very well-built red that goes well with roasted or grilled red meats.

NOTES
....
....
....
....

★ ★ ★ ★

Château de Vaugelas 'Le Prieuré' Corbières 2011

AOC CORBIERES $13.70 (361691) **XD**

A blend of grenache, syrah and old-vine carignan, this is full of ripe, concentrated fruit from attack to medium finish. There's good complexity and structure, and the acidity comes through the fruit, lightening its depth and providing a texture that verges on juicy. Medium bodied and easygoing in tannins, it's a good choice for well-seasoned red meats and sausages.

NOTES

....
....
....
....

★ ★ ★ ★

Château Ducla 2011

AOC BORDEAUX SUPÉRIEUR $15.95 (255067) **XD**

"Ducla" is a corruption of "Douglas," the name of a former owner of the fourteenth-century building on the winery property that's shown on the label. This is a blend of cabernet sauvignon and merlot, and it shows solid fruit from start to finish, good complexity and concentration and effectively balanced acidity. The tannins are moderate and drying, and it's a very good choice for roast beef and other red meats.

NOTES

....
....
....
....

★ ★ ★ ★

Château Joinin 2009

AOC BORDEAUX $18.35 (305524) **D**

This is a very good example of a generic Bordeaux, this time made from merlot (90 percent) and cabernet franc. The fruit is well layered, with a clear ripe core, and the flavours hold true right through the palate. The tannins are easygoing to moderate, and the fruit–acid balance is right. You can pair this with roasted and grilled meats, and it will easily stretch to pork and richer poultry dishes.

NOTES

....
....
....
....

Château Pey la Tour 'Réserve du Château' 2009

★ ★ ★ ★ ½

AOC BORDEAUX SUPÉRIEUR $19.95 (925859) **XD**

[Vintages Essential] Bordeaux has special status among wines, but you don't always need to take out a second mortgage to buy a good one. This merlot-dominant blend (89 percent, with 8 percent cabernet sauvignon and 3 percent petit verdot) is smooth and clean textured with complex and concentrated flavours. It's medium bodied and dry with firm tannins, and it has very good balance. It's a lovely wine and an excellent dancing partner for red meats.

NOTES

....

....

....

NEW!

Château Pipeau Saint-Emilion Grand Cru 2011

★ ★ ★ ★ ★

AOC SAINT EMILION GRAND CRU $38.95   (302018)

[Vintages Essential] This is a blend of 90 percent merlot, and 5 percent each of cabernets sauvignon and franc. From one of Bordeaux's most prestigious appellations, it carries its pedigree well. Look for sculpted fruit that shows focus and definition, fine fruit–acid balance and well-calibrated supporting acidity. It's framed by supple tannins, and is a great partner for roasted and grilled red meats.

NOTES

....

....

....

....

Clos du Calvaire Châteauneuf-du-Pape 2011

★ ★ ★ ★ ½

AOC CHÂTEAUNEUF DU PAPE $32.40 (296855)   **D**

Mostly grenache, this delivers a lot of what you expect from a Châteauneuf-du-Pape: intense flavours, good acidity and drying tannins. The flavours here are broad and deep, with good layered complexity, the acidity comes close to juiciness, and the tannins are firm. With a sleek texture, this is made for red meats and is excellent with well-seasoned grilled lamb.

NOTES

....

....

....

....

Domaine du Petit Clocher Anjou 2012

★ ★ ★ ★ ½

AOC ANJOU $16.10 (293514) **XD**

Made of cabernet franc and from the Loire Valley, this is a terrific red.
Loire wines are generally underpriced (and underappreciated), and here
you get persistent, solid fruit flavours harnessed to juicy acidity. It's dry,
medium weight, lightly tannic and a great partner for red meats as well as
poultry and pork.

NOTES

....

....

....

....

....

E. Guigal Côtes du Rhône 2010

★ ★ ★ ★ ★

AOC CÔTES DU RHÔNE $17.95 (259721) **XD**

[Vintages Essential] There's so much mediocre côtes du Rhône about
that it's important to know which wines offer the best quality and value.
There's no doubt at all that this, from one of the most-respected producers
in the Rhône Valley, is one of them. It carries its concentrated flavour with
lightness and elegance, and the tangy texture is stylish. Medium bodied,
astringently dry and moderately tannic, it's an excellent choice for red
meats.

NOTES

....

....

....

François Labet 'Dame Alix' Côtes du Rhône 2012

★ ★ ★ ★

AOC CÔTES DU RHÔNE $11.95 (630657) **XD**

This is a blend of grenache, syrah and mourvèdre, three of the classic
grapes of this region, which spreads across a broad swath east of the River
Rhône near the Mediterranean. The wine has quite solid flavours, decent
complexity and a slightly tangy texture. It's dry and medium bodied with
moderate tannins. Drink it with pasta and tomato sauce, or with roast
chicken or turkey (with cranberries).

NOTES

....

....

....

....

NEW!
★ ★ ★ ★

Georges Duboeuf Brouilly 2011

AOC BROUILLY $17.95 (213934) **XD**

Brouilly is one of the recognized "crus" of Beaujolais, the top tier of the region. This one delivers solid and flavourful fruit, with nice complexity, right through the palate, and it's supported by bright and fresh acidity. Try it with a bottle of Beaujolais-Villages to appreciate the difference, and drink both with a poultry or pork dish.

NOTES

★ ★ ★ ★

Gérard Bertrand 'Réserve Spéciale' Cabernet Sauvignon 2011

IGP PAYS D'OC $14.00 (234815) **XD**

You might think that, coming from the warm South of France, this would be fruit forward and low in acid. The alcohol (14 percent) points that way, too. But in fact it's a very well-balanced cabernet, with concentrated but by no means overbearing flavours and fresh, clean acidity. The tannins are drying and sleek. It's a very good partner for red meats, but it also goes well with poultry and pork.

NOTES

★ ★ ★ ★ ½

Joseph Drouhin Côte de Beaune-Villages 2010

AOC COTE DE BEAUNE-VILLAGES $23.95 (325126) **XD**

This wine (made from pinot noir) comes from a number of villages around the city of Beaune (in Burgundy) that have been identified as making consistently superior wine. This one is quite lovely. It combines fruit that is ripe-sweet at the core and well layered, with a broad seam of fresh, clean acidity. It's medium bodied and very versatile at the table. Try it with poultry, pork and grilled salmon.

NOTES

★ ★ ★ ★

Jovly Chinon Cabernet Franc 2011

AOC CHINON $14.05 (300665) **D**

The cabernet francs of Chinon, in the Loire Valley, are well known
as some of the world's best examples of the variety. This is a very
approachable one, with fairly plush fruit, good complexity and nice
balance. It's medium bodied and soft textured, and goes as well with red
meats as with poultry and pork.

NOTES

....

....

....

....

★ ★ ★ ★

La Fiole Côtes du Rhône 2012

AOC CÔTES DU RHÔNE $15.00 (293498) **XD**

This is in the same funky bottle as the Châteauneuf-du-Pape (above), and
it's a very good example of the grenache/syrah blend from this well-known
region. It has a sleek and tangy texture, and the solid, consistent flavours
pair well with the fresh acidity. This is a very versatile red. Drink it with
red meats, poultry, pork, burgers and seasoned sausages.

NOTES

....

....

....

....

....

★ ★ ★ ★

La Fiole du Pape Châteauneuf-du-Pape

AOC CHÂTEAUNEUF-DU-PAPE $36.55   (12286) **D**

[Non-vintage] You can't miss the bottle. It's gnarled and twisted, with a
rough, gritty texture, as if it's been in a fire. But the wine's in very good
shape. It's a stylish red that has good structure and food-friendly balance.
Look for concentrated flavours with spicy accents and a tangy texture. It's
medium bodied and dry, with moderate tannins. Serve it with grilled or
roasted red meats.

NOTES

....

....

....

....

....

Les Jamelles Merlot 2012

★ ★ ★ ★

VIN DE PAYS D'OC $12.95 (245324) **D**

Merlot, one of the main red grapes of Bordeaux, is planted throughout the world. The vines that produced this are fairly close to home, in southern France, and they've come up with a style that's plush and rich in texture and flavour. Look for good concentration, a diversity of nuances and very good acid–fruit balance. It's a no-brainer for red meats, but it extends to pork, too.

NOTES
....
....
....
....

Les Volets Malbec 2011

★ ★ ★ ★

IGP HAUTE VALLEE DE L'AUDE $10.70 (332973) **XD**

Although malbec is now closely identified with Argentina, its home is southwest France, where this example comes from. It shows great flavours of ripe fruit, concentrated and complex, with a generous texture verging on juicy and tannins with a little grip. It's a terrific choice for red meats (beef and lamb spring to mind) and well-seasoned grilled sausages.

NOTES
....
....
....
....

Louis Bernard Côtes du Rhône Villages 2012

★ ★ ★ ★

AOC CÔTES DU RHÔNE VILLAGES $15.10 (391458) **XD**

The appellation means that the wine comes from villages within the côtes du Rhône that are recognized as making superior wine. This one is mostly a blend of grenache and syrah, and it delivers lovely flavours that are focused and consistent right through the palate. Look for a refreshing texture and easygoing tannins, and drink this with red meats, pork, veal and well-seasoned sausages.

NOTES
....
....
....
....

★ ★ ★ ★

Louis Jadot Bourgogne Pinot Noir 2012

AOC BOURGOGNE $22.95 (162073) **XD**

Pinot noir is the signature grape of Burgundy, where it's made in many (often subtly different) styles. This example is affordably mid-range. It's medium bodied and very dry, with nicely managed fruit that delivers consistent flavours from start to finish. The tannins are easygoing and the acidity adds a refreshing texture. It goes well with grilled salmon, poultry, pork and tomato-based vegetarian dishes.

NOTES

....

....

....

....

★ ★ ★ ★

Louis Jadot 'Combe aux Jacques' Beaujolais-Villages 2011

AOC BEAUJOLAIS-VILLAGES $17.95 (365924) **D**

[Vintages Essential] Light in tannins, beaujolais (which is made from the gamay variety) is often a good choice for anyone who finds that red wines lead to a headache. This one is quite classic: medium bodied and dry with bright fruit flavours, some complexity and a vibrant, refreshing texture. You can serve it slightly chilled, especially in the summer, with roast or grilled chicken or with roast turkey.

NOTES

....

....

....

★ ★ ★ ★

Louis Latour Pinot Noir 2012

AOC BOURGOGNE $19.95 (69914) **XD**

This is a reliable red burgundy, now labelled "pinot noir" to help consumers who buy by grape variety, not wine region. It's in one of the classic Burgundy styles: fairly light in colour but with surprising depth and complexity in the flavours, a tangy and refreshing texture and drying tannins. It's a great choice for roast poultry and cranberries or for grilled salmon.

NOTES

....

....

....

....

....

Mas des Montagnes 2010
NEW!
★ ★ ★ ★

CÔTES DU ROUSSILLON VILLAGES $13.60 (361618) **XD**

A blend of grenache, syrah and carignan, this is medium-plus in body, and is packed with attractive fruit. It's dry, with moderate and manageable tannins. The flavours show some complexity and good consistency, and there's plenty of acidity to suit it for food. Try it with many red meats, hearty stews and well-seasoned sausages, or with burgers from the grill.

NOTES

....

....

....

....

....

M. Chapoutier Rasteau 2012
NEW!
★ ★ ★ ★ ½

AOC RASTEAU $19.50   (321539)   **D**

Rasteau is one of the villages singled out as producing superior wines within the côtes du Rhône appellation. Made from grenache and syrah, it has intense aromas and delivers generous and concentrated flavours. The well-calibrated acidity shines through as very attractive juiciness, and the wine, while very dry, is only lightly tannic. It's an excellent choice for braised beef and for red meats in general.

NOTES

....

....

....

....

Michel Lynch Bordeaux Merlot 2011
NEW!
★ ★ ★ ★ ½

AOC BORDEAUX $17.75 (361550) **XD**

This is a very attractive merlot-dominant wine that delivers good quality across the board. The fruit is concentrated but understated, with structure and complexity to spare. The acidity is spot-on, calibrated to freshen up the fruit, and the tannins have a little grip but are easily managed. This is an excellent choice for roasted and grilled red meats and hearty stews.

NOTES

....

....

....

....

Mommessin 'Les Épices' Châteauneuf-du-Pape 2010

★ ★ ★ ★ ½

AOC CHÂTEAUNEUF-DU-PAPE $30.00 (42242) **XD**

Châteauneuf-du-Pape is an iconic appellation in the southern Rhône Valley, near Avignon. The wines can be made from many different varieties, but most, like this one, draw mainly on grenache. Here you'll find richness and complexity of flavour, big body and real depth to the smooth texture. The tannins are firm but manageable. This calls for food with heft, like lamb and beef.

NOTES

....
....
....
....

Ogier 'Heritages' Côtes du Rhône 2011

★ ★ ★ ★

AOC CÔTES DU RHÔNE $14.95 (535849) **D**

This is a solid and reliable southern Rhône blend of grenache, syrah and mourvèdre. There's plenty of flavour here, some complexity and decent structure. It's dry, medium bodied and nicely balanced, with a good tangy texture and moderate tannins. Try it with grilled or roasted red meats, paella and coq au vin.

NOTES

....
....
....
....
....

Paul Jaboulet Aîné 'Parallèle 45' 2010

★ ★ ★ ★

CÔTES DU RHÔNE $16.05 (332304) **D**

This classic southern Rhône blend of grenache (60 percent) and syrah (40 percent) delivers good, solid flavours from start to finish. They're nicely complex and structured, and they're well integrated with the broad seam of clean acidity that shines through and makes the wine so successful with food. This is versatile at the table, and will stretch from lamb to poultry and pork.

NOTES

....
....
....
....

★ ★ ★ ★

Paul Mas 'Nicole Vineyard' Cabernet Sauvignon/Merlot 2012

IGP PAYS D'OC $13.95 (293134) **D**

Look for well-concentrated, even intense, fruit flavours in this wine. They show good complexity and structure, and they pair well with clean, fresh acidity. It's quite mouth filling, dense and fairly smooth with an interesting edge, and the tannins are ripe and drying. This is a very good choice for red meat dishes and is perfect for well-seasoned grilled steak.

NOTES
....
....
....
....

★ ★ ★ ★ ★

Perrin & Fils 'Les Sinards' Châteauneuf-du-Pape 2011

AOC CHÂTEAUNEUF-DU-PAPE $34.95 (926626) **XD**

[Vintages Essential] 'Les Sinards' is a sort of junior Château de Beaucastel, an iconic wine from this region, but it surrenders nothing to quality. Made mainly from grenache, with syrah and mourvèdre playing minor roles, this is simply opulent, with fleshy, plush and layered fruit, finely tuned acidity and supple tannins. From an excellent vintage, this goes well with lamb and other red meats, suitably seasoned.

NOTES
....
....
....
....

★ ★ ★ ★ ★

Perrin Réserve Côtes du Rhône 2011

AOC CÔTES DU RHÔNE $15.95 (363457) **D**

[Vintages Essential] There's tremendous value in this bottle, vintage after vintage. It's a blend of grenache, syrah, mourvèdre and cinsault, made by the producer of Château de Beaucastel, an iconic Châteauneuf-du-Pape. This côtes du Rhône delivers rich, luscious flavours with an astonishingly intense, smooth and mouth-filling texture. Dry and well structured with good tannic grip, it's a great choice for grilled or roasted red meats.

NOTES
....
....
....
....

★ ★ ★ ★   **Philippe de Rothschild Cabernet Sauvignon 2012**

IGP PAYS D'OC $11.95   (407551) **XD**

Bold and concentrated, this is a step up in complexity and style from most reds at this price. The fruit is layered and defined, the fruit–acid balance is very good, and quite firm tannins frame everything. Dry and a bit more than medium bodied, it looks very good for grilled red meats, spicy sausages and burgers.

NOTES

....

....

....

....

....

NEW!
★ ★ ★ ★   **Roche Bastide Côtes du Rhône 2011**

AOC CÔTES DU RHÔNE $14.95 (360966) **XD**

This is a blend of grenache (70 percent) and syrah (30 percent), with the grapevines cultivated organically (without artificial fertilizers or pesticides). It's a very attractive blend that shows ripe fruit layered throughout the palate, with the right balance of fruit and acid. The texture is fresh but solid, and the tannins easily managed. Enjoy it with roasted lamb and other red meats.

NOTES

....

....

....

....

NEW!
★ ★ ★ ★   **Villa Ponciago Beaujolais-Villages 2012**

AOC BEAUJOLAIS-VILLAGES $15.30 (325134) **XD**

Beaujolais-Villages wines are what they sound like: wines produced in specific villages in the region that are recognized as making consistently superior beaujolais. This one has concentrated fruit that's well layered, and is bright and serious. The acidity is well calibrated, lending a fresh, juicy texture. It's very dry, and makes a great partner for poultry and pork. Think of it for roast turkey and cranberries.

NOTES

....

....

....

....

GERMANY

GERMANY IS FAR BETTER KNOWN for white wine than red, but actually produces reds in many of its regions, and pinot noir is becoming an increasingly important variety. Because of the cool climate and relatively short growing season, Germany's pinots tend to be in a lighter and crisper style.

Important terms on German wine labels are *Prädikatswein* (the highest-quality classification of wine) and *Qualitätswein* (sometimes followed by *b.A.*, designating wines of quality but not of the highest level). Each of these terms is followed by the name of the wine region where the grapes were grown.

Villa Wolf Pinot Noir 2012

★ ★ ★ ★

QUALITÄTSWEIN PFALZ $14.95   (291971)   **D**

Made in a lighter-bodied and dry style, this pinot noir goes well with
grilled or roast poultry, roast pork and grilled salmon, and will pair
nicely with many summer salads. The flavours are understated, solid right
through the palate and nicely layered, and they are complemented by
bright, pleasant acidity.

NOTES

....

....

....

....

GREECE

THE HOT GROWING CONDITIONS IN GREECE make for full-flavoured reds. Although many are produced from native grape varieties, notably agiorgitiko (sometimes called St. George), international varieties such as cabernet sauvignon are also making headway. An AOC-designated wine from Greece means that it complies with the laws regulating wine quality.

Boutari Agiorgitiko 2011

★ ★ ★ ★

PDO NEMEA $11.95   (172148) **XD**

The agiorgitiko grape variety (also known as St. George) is native to Greece, and here it makes a wine that goes well with roast chicken, turkey and pork, and easily extends to many burgers and pizzas. It's on the light side of medium bodied, but delivers well-focused flavours and well-balanced acidity with easygoing tannins.

NOTES

....

....

....

....

Hatzimichalis Cabernet Sauvignon 2009

★ ★ ★ ★

REGIONAL WINE OF ATALANTI VALLEY $17.95   (538074) **D**

This is a quite powerful and very attractive cabernet sauvignon made in an international style. Look for bold, intense flavours that are echoed in the big, mouth-filling texture. This is a full-bodied cabernet that's dry and still quite tannic, with a good seam of acidity that suits it for food. Serve it with grilled red meats, like lamb or beef, cooked medium rare at most and served with lemon wedges.

NOTES

....

....

....

....

ITALY

ITALY HAS LONG PRODUCED RED WINES from native grape varieties, but in recent years international varieties like merlot and cabernet sauvignon have also been planted. There are many regional varieties, the best known being sangiovese, originally from Tuscany and now grown and used in winemaking throughout Italy. Other important varieties are nero d'Avola from Sicily and primitivo from southern Italy.

The highest-quality classification of Italian wines is DOCG (*Denominazione di Origine Controllata e Garantita*), which indicates a wine made to stringent regulations and from a few specified grape varieties. Wines in the next category, DOC (*Denominazione di Origine Controllata*), follow similar rules. Wines labelled IGT (*Indicazione Geografica Tipica*) or IGP (*Indicazione Geografica Protetta*) are made according to less stringent regulations and may use a wider range of grape varieties. This doesn't mean that a DOCG wine is necessarily better than an IGT/IGP— in fact, some of Italy's most famous wines are IGT/IGP wines. Overall, you'll find quality and value in all these categories, as this list shows.

Ascheri Barbera d'Alba 2011

DOC BARBERA D'ALBA $15.80 (219790) **XD**

Barbera is a too-little-known grape variety. Taste this lovely wine and you'll find that it delivers high-toned and concentrated flavours from start to finish, with a well-tuned texture that's fresh and lively. It's dry with light tannins, and it makes a great partner for many tomato-based Italian dishes (pizza, pasta, meats) as well as for pork, chicken and turkey dishes.

NOTES

....

....

....

....

NEW!
★ ★ ★ ★ ½

Ascheri Barolo 2009

DOCG BAROLO $33.80 (341107) **XD**

Made from nebbiolo grapes in the Barolo region of Piedmont, this is a powerful wine that's remarkably light on its feet, and very food friendly. Look for real depth in the ripe flavours that show structure and complexity. With good fruit–acid balance and supple tannins, this is a natural for full-flavoured red meat dishes.

NOTES

....

....

....

....

★ ★ ★ ★ ½

Batasiolo Barolo 2009

DOCG BAROLO $29.95 (178541) **XD**

Barolo is considered one of Italy's great wines. Made from the nebbiolo variety in Piedmont, it's typically big, intense and very smooth. This one fits the description very well. You'll find real flavour intensity with layered complexity and structure, together with a texture that's a tense combination of plush and fresh. The tannins are supple and it's ready for grilled or roasted red meats and game.

NOTES

....

....

....

....

....

Bersano 'Costalunga' Barbera d'Asti 2012

★ ★ ★ ★

DOCG BARBERA D'ASTI $12.00   (348680)   **D**

Made 100 percent from barbera grapes, this is a widely versatile wine for food. Try it with burgers and pizza, red meats and poultry, pasta dishes and pork. Barbera is often like that when it's made in this style: dry and medium bodied with solid and concentrated fruit, but understated rather than forward, with good balancing acidity and moderate tannins.

NOTES

....

....

....

....

....

Bolla Amarone della Valpolicella Classico 2008

NEW!
★ ★ ★ ★ ½

DOC AMARONE DELLA VALPOLICELLA CLASSICO

$36.95   (352757)   **D**

Amarone often impresses because it is such a big-bodied and deeply flavourful wine. But with the heft you also need what this example offers: complexity, structure and balance. It's the difference between a wine that kills food and wine that complements it. This has it all, and although the tannins are firm (you could easily keep it until 2018), it's drinking well now. Pair it with well-seasoned red meat dishes.

NOTES

....

....

....

Bolla Valpolicella Classico 2012

★ ★ ★ ★

DOC VALPOLICELLA CLASSICO $12.95   (16840)   **D**

Valpolicella is a wine region in the Veneto, in northeastern Italy, and all valpolicella wines are red. The most common grape is corvina, an Italian variety, and here it makes for a straightforward and very drinkable wine that's excellent for tomato-based pasta, meat and vegetable dishes. Look for well-focused fruit flavours and a juicy texture from the supporting acidity.

NOTES

....

....

....

Bonacchi Brunello di Montalcino 2007

★ ★ ★ ★ ½

DOCG BRUNELLO DI MONTALCINO $35.80 (266965) **XD**

This powerful wine is driven by a clone of the sangiovese variety. Here it makes for full-on flavours that are intense, well focused and have very good structure. The acidity shines though, keeping it fresh and holding the weight of the fruit in check, and the tannins are drying. This is a big wine for big food. Drink it with well-seasoned steak or grilled game.

NOTES
....
....
....
....
....

Borgo Bello Bolgheri 2010

NEW!
★ ★ ★ ★ ½

DOC BOLGHERI $18.80 (341123) **D**

Bogheri is the appellation of a number of Super Tuscan wines, and this blend of cabernet sauvignon, sangiovese and merlot fits the region well. It's an intensely flavoured wine, characterized by deep fruit and spiciness, and shows very good structure and complexity. The texture is round and full, quite smooth, and the tannins are drying and manageable. This is wine for well-seasoned red meats and game.

NOTES
....
....
....
....

Campo Maccione Morellino di Scansano 2010

★ ★ ★ ★

DOCG MORELLINO DI SCANSANO $13.95 (253831) **D**

From a small appellation in Tuscany, this is a very attractive blend of sangiovese (known as morellino in the area), cabernet, merlot and syrah. It has a very fresh, vibrant texture, and the flavours are equally lively. It's dry, with moderate tannins, and is very versatile with food. Try it with tomato-based fish stews, chicken, pork and (of course) many Italian dishes.

NOTES
....
....
....
....

Carione Brunello di Montalcino 2006

★ ★ ★ ★ ½

DOCG BRUNELLO DI MONTALCINO $30.05 (266668) **XD**

This is a very stylish red and a rare brunello (a clone of sangiovese grown in the Montalcino region) that's available year-round in Ontario. Look for elegance here, a texture that's generous, smooth and yet high-toned. The flavours are focused and subtly layered, and the tannins are there and supple. Well integrated, it goes well with red meats and full-flavoured Italian dishes.

NOTES

....
....
....
....

Casa Planeta Syrah 2012

★ ★ ★ ★ ★

DOC SICILIA $11.95 (219857) **XD**

This very attractive syrah delivers a generous, juicy texture that suits it to many different foods. Try it with chicken or turkey, lamb or beef, pork or veal, or burgers or pizzas. The flavours are focused and concentrated, there's a good spine of fresh acidity and the tannins are drying but not obtrusive. All the components hold together extremely well.

NOTES

....
....
....
....
....

Casal Thaulero Sangiovese 2012

★ ★ ★ ★

IGP TERRE DI CHIETI $7.45   (588996) **D**

This is a very attractive sangiovese. It has all the character you want from the grape—refreshing texture and fresh fruit flavour—but it has a bit more depth and complexity than most others around this low, low price. Look for bright flavours, a juicy texture and medium body. It's dry with light tannins, and it goes well with spaghetti bolognese, vegetarian lasagna and many pizzas.

NOTES

....
....
....
....

CastelGiocondo Brunello di Montalcino 2008

★ ★ ★ ★ ★

DOCG BRUNELLO DI MONTALCINO $49.95 (650432) **XD**

[Vintages Essential] This elegant, stylish wine is made from sangiovese grapes and aged in barrels for three years. You'll find that the flavours are dense, deep and broad, with multi-layered complexity and firm tannins. All this is supported by a solid platform of acidity that cuts through the weight of the fruit and makes for a tangy, fresh texture that invites you back to the glass. This is a big wine for big, well-seasoned food.

NOTES
....
....
....
....

Cent'Are Nero d'Avola/Merlot 2010

★ ★ ★ ★

IGP SICILIA $11.95 (323543) **XD**

This blend replaces the Cent'Are single-variety nero d'Avola that was in the LCBO for many years. The "black grape of Avola" is native to Sicily and makes wines with intense flavours and colour. The blend shows solid, concentrated flavours and moderate tannins, with a winning texture that's lively and fresh. Drink this with vegetarian or meat-based dishes in a tomato sauce.

NOTES
....
....
....
....

Cesari Amarone Classico 2009

★ ★ ★ ★ ½

DOC AMARONE DELLA VALPOLICELLA CLASSICO

$37.95 (426718) **D**

This has all the structure and defined flavours you expect from a well-made amarone. It's deep and broad, with layers of pungent, vibrant and mature flavours that come on in waves. The texture is rich, tangy, mouth filling and surprisingly lively given the weight of the wine. Dry, full bodied and delicious, this amarone calls for substantial and well-seasoned red meat dishes, like a rosemary/garlic rack of lamb or pepper steak.

NOTES
....
....
....

Cesari 'Mara' Valpolicella Superiore Ripasso 2010

★ ★ ★ ★ ½

DOC VALPOLICELLA SUPERIORE $17.95 (506519) **XD**

This is a big, dense red with a plush, smooth texture that's a good choice when you're grilling red meats, game or richly flavoured sausages. It has attractive and full-flavoured fruit and good complexity. The tannins are moderate and drying, and although it's lower in acidity than you might expect, there's some distinct juiciness to the texture.

NOTES
....
....
....
....
....

Citra Montepulciano d'Abruzzo 2012

★ ★ ★ ★

DOP MONTEPULCIANO D'ABRUZZO $7.45   (446633) **D**

Like many Italian wine names, this combines a grape variety (montepulciano) and a wine region (Abruzzo). This is a surprisingly well-made and attractive wine for the price. You get rich, concentrated flavours that flow through consistently from start to finish. It might not be all that complex, but the texture—tangy and refreshing—is very appealing, and this is ideal for grilled red meats and hearty tomato-based vegetarian stews.

NOTES
....
....
....
....

Costa Mediana Valpolicella Ripasso 2011

NEW!
★ ★ ★ ★ ½

DOC VALPOLICELLA RIPASSO $16.95 (377648) **D**

This is an impressive new wine in the LCBO's lineup. It comes with dense, layered and defined flavours that are well structured and consistent right through the palate. The spine of fresh acidity shines through and lightens the fruit, and the tannins are moderate and supple. This is a wine for well-seasoned red and game meats, whether roasted or grilled.

NOTES
....
....
....

Cusumano Nero d'Avola 2012

★ ★ ★ ★

IGT TERRE SICILIANE $10.95 (143164) **XD**

Sicily is coming to the fore with some high-quality and many good-value wines. This is one of the latter, made from the indigenous variety that's become the island's signature grape. Here you get quite intense flavours with limited complexity and good consistency, and an attractive tangy texture. With moderate tannins, it's a good bet for well-flavoured red meats and pasta dishes.

NOTES

....

....

....

....

Doppio Passo Primitivo 2012

★ ★ ★ ★

IGT SALENTO $9.95 (255190) **D**

This is a nicely made, straightforward primitivo from the south of Italy. It shows ripe sweetness at the core of the fruit, a fairly smooth texture and good acid–fruit balance. It's dry with easygoing tannins. You can't go wrong pairing this with grilled seasoned sausages, burgers, ribs and many pasta dishes.

NOTES

....

....

....

....

....

Enrico Serafino Barbaresco 2010

NEW!
★ ★ ★ ★ ½

DOCG BARBARESCO $21.85 (341156) **XD**

Made from the nebbiolo variety, this is a very attractive red that goes well with many red meats, as well as with hearty Italian cuisine (like osso buco). Look for rich, intense flavours with real breadth and complexity, supported by acidity that is clean, fresh and delivers juiciness to the texture. The tannins are easygoing, and all the components are well integrated.

NOTES

....

....

....

....

★ ★ ★ ★ ½ **Farina 'Le Pezze' Ripasso Valpolicella Classico Superiore 2011**

DOC VALPOLICELLA CLASSICO SUPERIORE $15.95 (195966)   D

The name is quite a mouthful, but then, so is the wine. The flavours are rich and dense, with depth and complexity, and the texture is fleshy and generous. The acidity provides a nice counterbalance, weighing in with life and freshness. The tannins are moderate. This is a very good wine to go with steak Florentine, and with red meats and rich pastas in general.

NOTES

....

....

....

....

★ ★ ★ ★ ½ **Farnese 'Casale Vecchio' Montepulciano d'Abruzzo 2011**

DOC MONTEPULCIANO D'ABRUZZO $10.95   (612788)   D

This is a very impressive wine, with flavours that are sweet, rich and dense but well defined, and with good complexity. It's dense and mouth filling in texture, but the acidity is well integrated and leaves your palate feeling saturated but refreshed. Dry and full bodied, it's a great choice for meat-rich Italian dishes and for any red meat and hearty stew.

NOTES

....

....

....

....

....

★ ★ ★ ★ **Farnese Negroamaro 2011**

IGT PUGLIA $8.95   (143735)   D

Negroamaro ("black bitter") is a variety indigenous to Puglia, in the south of Italy, where this wine comes from. Despite the name, this wine is deep red (not black) and full of sweet and ripe (not bitter) flavours. It has very good acidity, is dry with easygoing tannins and is a great choice for casual meals of pasta, burgers and many red meats.

NOTES

....

....

....

....

....

Farnese Sangiovese 2012

★ ★ ★ ★

IGT DAUNIA $7.95   (512327)   **D**

When this wine first hit the LCBO's shelves some years ago, its price/quality combination made it an instant hit. It flew off the shelves and the LCBO had trouble keeping it in stock. It's still very good value, even though it's climbed slightly in price. Look for bright and vibrant flavours, medium weight and a refreshing texture. You can't go wrong serving this with pizza and tomato sauce–based pasta.

NOTES

....

....

....

....

Folonari Valpolicella Ripasso Classico Superiore 2011

★ ★ ★ ★

DOC VALPOLICELLA RIPASSO CLASSICO SUPERIORE

$17.95   (481838)   **D**

To make a ripasso wine, the wine is fermented on the skins left over from making amarone, which itself is made from dried grapes. This gives ripasso wines more depth and complexity, and you can taste and feel the effects here. There's very good concentration, lots of complexity, firm and drying tannins and very good acidity. This is an excellent choice for hearty Italian food.

NOTES

....

....

....

Fontanafredda Barolo 2009

★ ★ ★ ★ ½

DOCG BAROLO $30.00   (20214)   **XD**

This is a gorgeous wine, one of those winners that combines power and depth with elegance and style. The fruit flavours are concentrated and nicely structured, and they're complemented by refreshing and well-calibrated acidity. The tannins are firm and ripe, and the wine is a great choice if you're having osso bucco or any meat in a tomato-based sauce.

NOTES

....

....

....

....

....

Fontanafredda 'Briccotondo' Barbera 2012
★ ★ ★ ★ ½
DOC PIEMONTE $15.95 (72348) XD

[Vintages Essential] Barbera is a variety that deserves to be more popular. Take this example, which delivers great flavours that are layered and serious but fresh and vibrant. The acidity is pitched right—forward and juicy but not at all harsh—and the tannins are drying but in the background. It's a perfect wine for mushroom risotto or any tomato-based Italian dish.

NOTES

Frescobaldi 'Rèmole' Toscana 2012
NEW!
★ ★ ★ ★
IGT TOSCANA $12.95 (105429) D

This is a blend of sangiovese (85 percent) and cabernet sauvignon (the rest), and together they make for flavours that are well concentrated without being intense, and well defined. The fruit is supported by bright, refreshing acidity, and this is one of those Italian wines that goes well with the usual sangiovese suspects: tomato-based pasta and meat dishes of all kinds.

NOTES

Gabbiano Chianti 2012
★ ★ ★ ★
DOCG CHIANTI $13.95 (78006) XD

The grapes for this dry, medium-weight wine are from the estate of the Castello di Gabbiano, a thirteenth-century castle located on a hill in chianti classico country. In the bottle you'll find attractive flavours that are solid, fresh and concentrated, with good complexity. They're complemented by a tangy and refreshing texture and great balance, and this goes very well with a rich, tomato-based pasta or any stew in a red wine and tomato sauce.

NOTES

Gabbiano Chianti Classico 2010

★ ★ ★ ★ ★

DOCG CHIANTI CLASSICO $16.95 (219808) **XD**

"Classico" means that the grapes for the wine came from the area that was originally demarcated for chianti; it has been expanded over time. This example delivers lovely rich and focused flavours with impressive complexity and range. They're complemented and supported by fresh acidity that gives a sleek and refreshing texture, and framed by supple tannins. Drink it with classic Italian dishes.

NOTES

....

....

....

....

Luccarelli Primitivo 2012

★ ★ ★ ★

IGP PUGLIA $10.40 (253856) **D**

Less expensive primitivo—the variety now associated with the southern region of Puglia—can be intense and heavy. This one achieves real lightness of being and brings a juicy texture without sacrificing the concentration of flavour. It's very attractive and, more important, very drinkable wine, and goes well with many tomato-based dishes as well as poultry and pork.

NOTES

....

....

....

....

Masi Campofiorin 2010

★ ★ ★ ★ ★

IGT ROSSO DEL VERONESE $19.95 (155051) **XD**

Campofiorin is a stylish wine that's reliable year after year. It's made by adding freshly fermented wine to the grape skins that remain after the super-rich amarone is made. The result has dense, intense flavours of complex, ripe fruit. It's more than medium bodied, and dry with a tangy texture. It's a real treat to drink and goes well with spicy pasta dishes with grated Parmigiano Reggiano.

NOTES

....

....

....

....

★ ★ ★ ★ ½ Masi 'Costasera' Amarone della Valpolicella Classico 2009

DOC AMARONE DELLA VALPOLICELLA CLASSICO

$39.95 (317057) **D**

Amarone is made from grapes that are allowed to dry on bamboo mats for a few months before being pressed. The drying process leads to more concentrated flavours and complexity, as this wine shows. Its layers of ripe and mature fruit are dense and well focused, and it has an opulent texture. Dry and moderately tannic with a tangy texture, it's an excellent choice for rich red meat dishes and aged hard cheeses.

NOTES

★ ★ ★ ★ Masi Serego Alighieri 'Possessioni Rosso' 2011

IGT ROSSO DEL VERONESE $15.00 (447326) **D**

Masi is a well-known producer of quality wines, and this delicious red blend (mainly corvina and sangiovese grape varieties) shows the value it offers, too. This has concentrated and nicely nuanced flavours, and you'll find the texture attractive and juicy. Medium bodied and dry, it's a natural candidate for Italian dishes, from vegetarian pizza to veal scaloppini.

NOTES

NEW! ★ ★ ★ ★ MezzoMondo Sangiovese/Merlot 2012

IGT PUGLIA $8.95 (79327) **D**

Look for plenty of flavour and good balance in this blend from the south of Italy. (Puglia is the heel of the Italian 'boot.') The fruit is bright, concentrated and focused, and the acidity lifts it effectively, giving the wine a fresh texture. The tannins are quite firm. Drink this with tomato-based pastas, pizza and many poultry or pork dishes.

NOTES

Montalto Nero d'Avola/Cabernet Sauvignon 2012

★ ★ ★ ★ ½

IGT SICILIA $8.95 (621151) **D**

For a long time, Sicily was better known for white wine than red, but in the last few years the reds, led by the native nero d'Avola grape variety, have been going gangbusters. Nero d'Avola is most of the blend here, and it delivers rich, complex flavours of dark fruit and spice. It's almost full bodied, with a generous and tangy texture. This is pretty big and needs the same kind of food, so pair it with well-seasoned red meat.

NOTES

....

....

....

....

Monte Antico 2009

★ ★ ★ ★ ½

IGT TOSCANA $15.95 (69377) **XD**

[Vintages Essential] This delicious wine is a blend of sangiovese—the signature red grape variety of Italy—merlot and cabernet sauvignon. It delivers robust and concentrated flavours that show complexity and depth, and a plush, full texture that's refreshing and tangy. A hint of rusticity adds to its attractiveness. This is an excellent wine for full-bodied Italian dishes, and it extends equally well to other rich meat and vegetarian cuisines.

NOTES

....

....

....

Montresor Amarone della Valpolicella 2010

NEW!
★ ★ ★ ★ ½

DOCG AMARONE DELLA VALPOLICELLA $39.75 (240416) **D**

Made from three grape varieties (corvina, rondinella, molinara), this delivers the intensity and style you would expect of an amarone. Look for concentrated, well-layered fruit that has both breadth and depth, complemented by a broad seam of clean, fresh acidity. The fruit is ripe-sweet and framed by supple tannins. It's an intensely flavoured wine that needs the same sort of food, so think of well-seasoned red meats and game.

NOTES

....

....

....

Negrar Amarone della Valpolicella Classico 2010

★ ★ ★ ★ ½

DOC AMARONE DELLA VALPOLICELLA CLASSICO

$36.95   (44784)   D

Plush, mouth filling and richly textured, this is a lovely amarone that delivers firm tannins and layers of concentrated flavour. It has just the right acidity needed to contain the richness of the fruit and make for a wine that pairs successfully with food. Enjoy this with any meal that features well-seasoned red meats. Alternatively, drink it with aged hard cheese such as Parmigiano Reggiano.

NOTES

....

....

....

NEW!

★ ★ ★ ★ ½

Pasqua Amarone della Valpolicella 2009

DOCG AMARONE DELLA VALPOLICELLA $34.85 (360958)   D

This bottle delivers the intensity and depth of flavour that's synonymous with amarone, but it does so gracefully and in style. The flavours are well structured, with good layering that radiates from the ripe-sweet core. The acidity complements the fruit and makes it very food-friendly, and the tannins are ripe and supple. Drink it with well-flavoured red meat and game dishes, or with full-flavoured, older cheeses.

NOTES

....

....

....

....

NEW!

★ ★ ★ ★ ½

Pasqua Passimento 2011

IGT VENETO $15.45   (141952)   D

The *appassimento* method of drying grapes before pressing them (to concentrate flavours) is used for amarone, but is being more and more widely employed. This example, made from corvina, croatina and merlot, is rich in flavour and big and generous in body. But it has the right degree of acidity to let you enjoy more than one glass. Pair it with substantial foods, like well-seasoned red meats.

NOTES

....

....

....

....

★ ★ ★ ★ ½

Pèppoli Chianti Classico 2011

DOCG CHIANTI CLASSICO $19.95 (606541) **XD**

[Vintages Essential] This is a lovely chianti from the "Classico" district, the area that was originally designated as the Chianti region. Look for solid but bright flavours here, with good structure and plenty of complexity, well supported by a broad seam of clean acidity. It's dry, juicy and moderately tannic, and it's a great partner for substantial Italian dishes and steak with chimichurri.

NOTES

....

....

....

....

★ ★ ★ ★ ½

Rocca delle Macìe Chianti Classico 2011

DOCG CHIANTI CLASSICO $18.95 (741769) **XD**

[Vintages Essential] This is a long-time favourite chianti classico (the "classico" meaning the grapes came from the original Chianti region, which has been expanded over time). It's quite a young chianti, with bright and vibrant flavours and a lively texture, and you can hold it a few years. Dry and medium bodied, it goes well with Italian tomato-based dishes, whether pasta, meat or pizza.

NOTES

....

....

....

....

★ ★ ★ ★ ½

Rocca delle Macìe 'Vernaiolo' Chianti 2012

DOCG CHIANTI $13.95 (269589) **XD**

The Chianti wine region produces tens of millions of bottles of wine a year, some of it exquisite, some of it not. (If you're old enough to have been drinking chianti in the 1960s and 1970s, you'll remember some of the not-exquisite chiantis in wicker baskets.) Vernaiolo is an attractive chianti with quite concentrated flavours of ripe fruit. It's dry, moderately tannic, juicy textured and perfect with chicken parmesan.

NOTES

....

....

....

....

THE 500 BEST-VALUE WINES IN THE LCBO | 2015

Ruffino Il Ducale Sangiovese-Merlot-Syrah 2012

★ ★ ★ ★ ½

IGT TOSCANA $19.00 (27797) XD

It might seem an unlikely blend for Tuscany, where sangiovese is king, but producers have been working cabernet sauvignon and merlot into blends with it for decades. This is a very good example, with vibrant but serious fruit, refreshing acidity, and moderate tannins. It holds together very well, and is a great choice for hearty stews and red meats cooked Italian-style.

NOTES
....
....
....
....
....

Ruffino 'Riserva Ducale' Chianti Classico 2010

★ ★ ★ ★ ★

DOCG CHIANTI CLASSICO RISERVA $24.95   (45195) D

This is a stylish chianti from the original Chianti zone of production. Look for ripe fruit flavours that have breadth, depth, definition and focus, harnessed to a broad seam of fresh acidity. With ripe tannins and a juicy texture, it's a great choice for steak Florentine, osso bucco and braised lamb.

NOTES
....
....
....
....
....
....

Sella & Mosca Riserva Cannonau di Sardegna 2009

NEW!
★ ★ ★ ★ ½

DOC CANNONAU DI SARDEGNA $16.95 (425488) XD

Cannonau is the Sardinian name for the grape variety more widely known as grenache. This example delivers concentrated fruit flavour from start to long finish, with plenty of complexity and excellent acid–fruit balance. It's very dry, and the tannins are moderate and manageable. It's an excellent partner for osso buco and for many lamb and other red meat dishes.

NOTES
....
....
....
....

Spinelli 'Quartana' Montepulciano d'Abruzzo 2011

★ ★ ★ ★

DOC MONTEPULCIANO D'ABRUZZO $7.50   (454629)   **D**

Made in the Abruzzo region from the montepulciano variety, this is one of those worthy under-$10 wines in the LCBO. You'll find a lot of food-friendly juiciness in the texture and plenty of concentrated ripe fruit in the flavours. It has decent complexity and good balance, and it's a no-brainer for many tomato-based pasta dishes, poultry and pork.

NOTES
....
....
....
....
....

Tedeschi Amarone della Valpolicella Classico 2009

★ ★ ★ ★ ½

DOC AMARONE DELLA VALPOLICELLA CLASSICO

$39.95 (433417) **D**

[Vintages Essential] The grapes for this wine are dried for four months, allowing them to shrivel and the water in them to evaporate. When they're finally pressed, the grapes have more concentrated flavours. The wine is then aged for two to three years in oak barrels and another six months in the bottle. Taste the process in the rich, intense, complex flavours and the almost decadently opulent texture. This needs big, rich food such as lamb, steak or game.

NOTES
....
....
....

Tini Sangiovese di Romagna 2012

★ ★ ★ ★

DOC SANGIOVESE DI ROMAGNA $9.95   (179432)   **D**

At this price, you can't go wrong with this wine when you're gathering friends for pizza or a meal of pasta. Made from sangiovese in the region of Romagna, it's a dry red with a texture that's concentrated and bright. The freshness of the acidity shows through nicely and complements the vibrant flavours, which are modestly complex but consistent from start to finish.

NOTES
....
....
....
....

Tommasi 'Il Sestante' Ripasso Valpolicella 2012

★ ★ ★ ★ ½

DOC VALPOLICELLA CLASSICO $16.95 (267070)   D

This is a very attractive and well-priced ripasso valpolicella that demonstrates the intensity the ripasso method contributes. The fruit is concentrated, well structured and nicely focused, and the acidity shines through with juicy freshness. The tannins are sweet and drying, and it's a great choice for poultry, pork and the usual Italian gastronomic suspects.

NOTES

....

....

....

....

....

Tommasi Ripasso Valpolicella Classico Superiore 2012

★ ★ ★ ★ ★

DOC VALPOLICELLA RIPASSO CLASSICO SUPERIORE

$22.95 (910430)   D

[Vintages Essential] This terrific valpolicella is a great choice for many hearty Italian-style dishes with a tomato base, as well as for well-seasoned poultry and pork. The fruit is serious but vibrant, well-defined and consistent, and its weight is lifted by clean and fresh acidity. The tannins are ripe and slightly gripping. In all, it's an impressive and versatile red.

NOTES

....

....

....

....

Umberto Fiore Barbaresco 2009

★ ★ ★ ★ ★

DOCG BARBARESCO $18.45 (254870) XD

Made from nebbiolo grapes in an appellation near Barbaresco in the region of Piedmont, this is a beautiful wine, characterized by poise and style. Already more than five years old, it shows maturing fruit flavours that are still lively and fresh, with vibrant acidity and drying tannins. It's medium bodied and a perfect choice for roast poultry, grilled duck and many medium- to strong-flavoured mature cheeses.

NOTES

....

....

....

Zenato Ripassa Valpolicella Superiore 2009

★ ★ ★ ★ ½

DOC VALPOLICELLA SUPERIORE RIPASSO $25.95 (479766) **D**

[Vintages Essential] Ripasso wine is made by fermenting it on the skins of grapes that have been used for making amarone. They give ripassos richness and complexity, as this one shows. The flavours are deep, broad, layered and solid, and they're complemented by clean acidity that translates as a tangy texture. It's a great choice for steaks, red meat roasts and full-flavoured aged cheeses.

NOTES

....

....

....

....

NEW ZEALAND

NEW ZEALAND IS BEST KNOWN for its white wine, especially sauvignon blancs from the Marlborough region in the South Island. But it turns out that New Zealand produces many very good red wines, too, including merlots from the North Island. Its pinot noirs are especially impressive, notably from Central Otago (the southernmost wine region in the world) and Marlborough, two regions in the South Island. Most are made in volumes too small for the LCBO General Purchase List, but we are seeing a better selection every year.

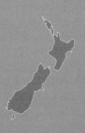

Kim Crawford Pinot Noir 2012

★ ★ ★ ★ ½

MARLBOROUGH $19.95 (626390) **XD**

[Vintages Essential] Kim Crawford is one of New Zealand's best-known winemakers, and here he lends his name to a very attractive pinot noir. From grapes grown in the very sunny but cool Marlborough wine region, it shows lovely focused and layered flavours that are harnessed to fresh acidity and framed by supple tannins. It's quite delicious and a great partner for roasted or grilled lamb.

NOTES

The People's Pinot Noir 2012

★ ★ ★ ★

CENTRAL OTAGO $16.95 (234526) **XD**

With its funky label, off-the-wall name and suggestion that you pair it with "film, fire and friends," your expectations of this wine might be low. In fact, it's a well-made pinot with good complexity and breadth in the ripe flavours, a fresh, juicy texture and supple, if modest, tannins. It's a good partner for grilled salmon and roast chicken or turkey.

NOTES

Stoneleigh Pinot Noir 2012

★ ★ ★ ★

MARLBOROUGH $19.95 (54353) **XD**

Marlborough is best known for the sauvignon blancs that stormed world markets in the 1990s, but in terms of varieties planted, it's quite diverse. This lovely pinot noir shows the region's versatility. It delivers quite pure fruit flavours that are complex and layered, and a lovely, rich tangy texture that's great for food. This pinot will go well with duck breast, grilled salmon, roast turkey and even roast lamb.

NOTES

Villa Maria 'Private Bin' Pinot Noir 2012

★ ★ ★ ★

MARLBOROUGH $21.95 (146548) **XD**

Pinot noir is a popular wine partly because it's versatile with food. Depending on style, it goes well with red meats, poultry, pork, many vegetarian dishes and some fish and seafood. This example shows intense flavours with some sweet notes, good complexity and the right acidity to make it juicy. Try it with roast duck or turkey, grilled salmon or mushroom risotto.

NOTES

....

....

....

....

Whitehaven Pinot Noir 2012

★ ★ ★ ★ ½

MARLBOROUGH $23.95 (245696) **XD**

This delicious pinot noir carries all the hallmarks of the common New Zealand style: plenty of concentrated fruit with layers of complexity and rich yet understated flavour, harnessed to bright, vibrant acidity. Dry and more than medium in body, this has more power than many in the LCBO. It goes well with rich poultry (like coq au vin) and pork dishes, and easily stretches to roasted red meats.

NOTES

....

....

....

....

RED WINES

ONTARIO

THE MOST SUCCESSFUL RED GRAPE VARIETIES in Ontario
are those that thrive and ripen in its cool climate. They include
gamay, pinot noir and cabernet franc. The best known of
Ontario's four wine regions is Niagara Peninsula (which is now
divided into a number of sub-regions). Lake Erie North Shore,
which is somewhat warmer, is also represented in this list.

Wine labelled VQA (Vintners Quality Alliance) followed by a
region is made only from grapes grown in that area. The VQA
classification also means that the wine has been tested and tasted
by a panel.

Most non-VQA wines in the Ontario section of the LCBO are
blends of a small proportion of Ontario and foreign wine. They
are not included in this book because the range varies greatly
from year to year, depending on the Ontario grape harvest.

Cave Spring Gamay 2012

★ ★ ★ ★ ½

VQA NIAGARA PENINSULA $15.95 (228569) **D**

Gamay grapes grow very successfully in the Niagara Peninsula, but it's a variety overlooked by too many wine drinkers. This one from Cave Spring is just lovely. It has bright flavours of fresh fruit, and very refreshing, clean acidity. It's dry and medium bodied, and the juiciness in the texture makes you want to eat. Drink it with roast chicken or baked ham. I like to serve it just slightly chilled.

NOTES

....

....

....

....

Cave Spring Pinot Noir 2011

★ ★ ★ ★

VQA NIAGARA PENINSULA $17.95 (417642) **XD**

Cave Spring built its reputation on riesling, but it fires on all varietal cylinders. This is a really fine-tasting pinot noir. Look for vibrant, well-layered fruit, a very clean and refreshing texture and drying but easygoing tannins. It's dry and medium bodied and an excellent match for roast turkey or chicken, poached salmon or a tomato-based vegetarian dish.

NOTES

....

....

....

....

....

Château des Charmes Cabernet Franc 2011

★ ★ ★ ★ ½

VQA NIAGARA-ON-THE-LAKE $13.95 (162602) **XD**

From a cool vintage in Ontario, this is a lovely cabernet franc that shows perfectly ripe fruit right through the palate. The flavours are layered, well structured and focused, and they sit in excellent balance with the fresh and clean acidity. The tannins are drying and easily approachable. Drink this with duck, poultry, pork, and many red meat dishes.

NOTES

....

....

....

....

....

Château des Charmes Gamay Noir 2012

★ ★ ★ ★ ½

VQA NIAGARA-ON-THE-LAKE $12.95   (57349) **XD**

Gamay is the grape variety used to make beaujolais, but this wine is more substantial than most generic beaujolais, and is another wine that makes the case that gamay should be Ontario's signature red grape variety. What you get are concentrated flavours enlivened by a food-friendly and very refreshing texture. It's medium bodied and dry, and it goes extremely well with roast turkey and cranberries, as well as chicken, pork and many pastas.

NOTES

....

....

....

Coyote's Run Five Mile Red 2012

★ ★ ★ ★

VQA NIAGARA PENINSULA $16.95 (283416) **XD**

This blend of pinot noir (32 percent), cabernet (30 percent), merlot (27 percent) and syrah (11 percent) is attractive, easy drinking and very versatile with food. It's medium weight and dry with light tannins, and the flavours are solid all the way through. With bright and refreshing acidity, this goes well with turkey, chicken and pork, but it also extends to roasted and grilled red meats.

NOTES

....

....

....

....

Coyote's Run Pinot Noir 2012

★ ★ ★ ★

VQA NIAGARA PENINSULA $19.95   (53090) **XD**

From a cool Niagara vintage, this is a fairly concentrated style of pinot noir that delivers plenty of flavour and is an excellent style for chicken, turkey and grilled salmon, and will extend to many lighter red meat dishes. The flavours offer good complexity and consistency, and the texture is quite juicy. The tannins are drying and easily handled.

NOTES

....

....

....

....

★ ★ ★ ★

Creekside Syrah 2012

VQA NIAGARA PENINSULA $15.95   (66654) **XD**

This warm vintage delivers consistent and complex flavours along with a refreshing and tangy texture that tilts it toward food. The acidity contributes near-juiciness to the texture, and the tannins are perceptible and easily manageable. You can easily pair this with roasted or grilled pork and poultry.

NOTES
....
....
....
....
....

NEW!
★ ★ ★ ★

Earth & Sky Pinot Noir 2011

VQA NIAGARA PENINSULA $15.95 (343368) **XD**

Made by Château des Charmes, this is a mid-range style that's very versatile with food; you can drink it with duck, chicken and turkey (it's an excellent candidate for Thanksgiving), as well as grilled salmon and aged, sharp cheeses. The flavours are focused and concentrated, the acidity adds a high tone to the texture, and the tannins are drying and easygoing.

NOTES
....
....
....
....
....

NEW!
★ ★ ★ ★

EastDell Gamay Noir 2012

VQA NIAGARA PENINSULA $13.95 (214890) **XD**

Call it "gamay noir" or simply "gamay," this variety is represented in a good range of styles by a number of Ontario wineries. This one is very fresh and juicy in texture, with a good attack of acidity to set you up for food. The flavours are bright, with decent complexity, and the tannins are imperceptible. Drink it with poultry or tomato-based pasta dishes.

NOTES
....
....
....
....
....

★ ★ ★ ★

Fielding Estate Red Conception 2012

VQA NIAGARA PENINSULA $18.95 (189183) **XD**

A blend of cabernet franc (68 percent), cabernet sauvignon (18 percent), syrah (8 percent) and petit verdot (6 percent), this is dry and medium bodied, with the cabernet franc shining through. It shows understated flavours and a fairly tangy, crisp texture. It goes well with red meats, and extends to roast poultry and pork.

NOTES

....

....

....

....

....

NEW!
★ ★ ★ ★ ½

Flat Rock Cellars Pinot Noir 2012

DOC TWENTY MILE BENCH $19.95 (1545) **XD**

[Vintages Essential] This is a lovely pinot noir that combines real approachability with structure and complexity. It makes drinking quality pinot noir a pleasure, even for consumers who tend toward easy-drinking styles. The flavours are attractive, concentrated and well defined, and the acidity shines through, giving the texture a rounded edge. It's very versatile with food. Try it with pork, poultry, lamb and grilled salmon.

NOTES

....

....

....

....

NEW!
★ ★ ★ ★

Grange of Prince Edward 'Trumpour's Mill' Pinot Noir 2009

VQA PRINCE EDWARD COUNTY $16.95 (230227) **XD**

This is a mid-range style of pinot noir that shows consistent, decently layered fruit from attack to finish, with well-balanced acidity that contributes freshness and near-juiciness to the texture. It's medium bodied and dry, with easygoing tannins, and it makes a very good partner for poultry, pork and grilled salmon.

NOTES

....

....

....

....

Henry of Pelham Baco Noir 2012

VQA ONTARIO $14.95 (270926) **M**

Although the LCBO rates this as Medium in sweetness, I would call it
Dry. It's definitely a fruity wine, but the acidity and tannins dry the fruit
out well. You'll find it has less of the funky baco stuff going on, and is
fairly mellow. With fresh acidity and solid fruit, it's a versatile red you can
drink with pork, poultry and many simply prepared red meats.

NOTES

....

....

....

....

....

★ ★ ★ ★ ½

Henry of Pelham Pinot Noir 2012

VQA NIAGARA PENINSULA $16.95 (013904) **XD**

Henry of Pelham is one of Niagara's mid-size quality wineries, run by the
affable Speck brothers (three of them). With great balance between the
fruit and acidity, this attractive pinot noir makes a successful partner for
grilled lamb, veal chops or well-herbed roast chicken. It's medium bodied,
with attractive and vibrant flavours and a juicy, refreshing texture.

NOTES

....

....

....

....

....

★ ★ ★ ★

Inniskillin Cabernet Franc 2011

VQA NIAGARA PENINSULA $14.95 (317016) **XD**

This is a very attractive style of cabernet franc. It's on the lighter side, but
shows well-concentrated fruit that's quite complex, defined and consistent
from start to finish. The acidity is fresh and well balanced with the fruit,
and the tannins are moderate and drying. It's a very good choice for
chicken and pork, and it extends to straightforward red meats.

NOTES

....

....

....

....

....

★ ★ ★ ★ **Jackson-Triggs Reserve**
Cabernet Franc/Cabernet Sauvignon 2012

VQA NIAGARA PENINSULA $13.95 (560680) **D**

These are two of the main red varieties of Bordeaux, and here they make for a medium-bodied and intensely flavoured red that's a very good choice for grilled red meats and other hearty dishes. The flavours are nicely focused and complex, and the texture is very dry—though juicy—with firm tannins.

NOTES

....

....

....

....

....

NEW!
★ ★ ★ ★ **Jackson-Triggs Reserve Meritage 2012**

VQA NIAGARA PENINSULA $13.95 (526228) **XD**

Meritage (rhymes with "heritage") is a brand used to designate a blend of the grapes authorized in bordeaux wines. This one combines cabernet sauvignon, merlot and cabernet franc, and it delivers a lot of plush, ripe fruit that's well complemented by refreshing acidity. The tannins are quite firm, so drink it with red meats cooked medium rare at most.

NOTES

....

....

....

....

NEW!
★ ★ ★ ★ **Pelee Island 'Lighthouse' Cabernet Franc 2012**

VQA ONTARIO $11.95 (145441) **XD**

This is an easy-drinking light to medium–bodied cabernet franc that captures the essence of the variety well. There's a good range of elements in the flavour profile, and the fruit itself is nicely understated. The tannins are ripe, supple and easygoing. This is a wine you can pair with poultry and pork, but it will extend to simple red meat dishes, too.

NOTES

....

....

....

....

NEW!
★ ★ ★ ★

Peninsula Ridge Merlot 2012

VQA NIAGARA PENINSULA $14.95   (61101) **D**

Cool-climate merlot is often very attractive, as it delivers more acidity than many merlots show. Here the acidity comes through with a tangy texture, verging on juicy, which gives the wine the edge it needs to be food-versatile. With flavours that are concentrated and decently complex, this merlot makes a very good partner for red meats, burgers and stews (meat or vegetarian), as well as for pork and poultry.

NOTES

....
....
....
....
....

NEW!
★ ★ ★ ★

Rosehall Run 'Defiant' Pinot Noir 2012

VQA ONTARIO $18.95 (307769) **XD**

This is a pinot with some verve and lively brightness. The fruit is solid and well-defined, and although the wine is well balanced, it's as if the acidity is the active ingredient, giving the wine a juicy texture. It's a wine that calls for food, and it goes well with poultry, pork, salmon and beet salad.

NOTES

....
....
....
....
....

★ ★ ★ ★ ½

Southbrook 'Connect' Organic Red 2012

VQA ONTARIO $15.95   (249565) **D**

This is a very well-made red from one of Niagara's more stunning wineries. It's organic, and made from roughly equal parts of cabernets franc and sauvignon as well as merlot. Look for a lovely soft but refreshing texture that supports fruit that's ripe, focused and quite complex. It's dry, with fairly firm tannins, and it goes well with red meats, pork and hearty vegetarian dishes.

NOTES

....
....
....
....

NEW!
★ ★ ★ ★

Staff Baco Noir 2012

VQA ONTARIO $14.95 (260422) **D**

Made by winemaker Sue-Ann Staff, this baco noir is juicy and fresh and a good wine to serve with either poultry or pork dishes, or with many tomato-based pastas. The somewhat funky flavours associated with baco noir are muted here, and this will probably appeal to a wider range of consumers than many bacos. It's dry, with easygoing tannins, and very nicely balanced.

NOTES
....
....
....
....

NEW!
★ ★ ★ ★

Union Noir 2012

VQA NIAGARA PENINSULA $15.95 (277632) **XD**

This is a blend of two varieties—pinot noir and gamay—that often have similarities when made as varietal wines. Blending them has tended to amplify the similarities, so here you get nicely focused, high-toned fruit and balanced, juicy acidity. It speaks food, through and through, and it goes well with poultry and pork, as well as grilled salmon.

NOTES
....
....
....
....

PORTUGAL

PORTUGAL IS BEST KNOWN FOR PORT, and it seems logical that some of its best red wines are made from grape varieties permitted in port. They tend to be full of flavour, assertive in texture and big bodied. This also means that Portuguese reds are mainly made from indigenous grapes, and producers have generally resisted planting international varieties such as cabernet sauvignon and syrah. Portugal is a good source for inexpensive reds, as the following list shows.

The name of a region following DOC (*Denominação de Origem Controlada*) signifies a designated Portuguese wine region.

Catedral Reserva Dão 2010

★ ★ ★ ★

DOC DÃO $11.15   (219816) **D**

There's plenty of flavour and a quite rich texture in this affordable blend of alfrocheiro, tinta roriz and touriga nacional, all grape varieties permitted in port. The fruit–acid balance is good and there's a decent degree of complexity and light tannins. Dry and more than medium bodied, it's a very good choice for well-seasoned, grilled and roasted red meats.

NOTES

....
....
....
....
....

Fonseca Periquita 'Original' 2012

★ ★ ★ ★

VINHO REGIONAL PENÍNSULA DE SETÚBAL $8.95   (25262) **XD**

Portugal turns out not only many higher-priced quality wines (some of which are in Vintages) but also many good, less-expensive wines like this. It's a three-way blend that delivers plenty of flavour, some complexity and good fruit–acid balance. You can't go wrong opening it with a burger, grilled seasoned and spicy sausages or a hearty pizza.

NOTES

....
....
....
....
....

NEW!

Foral Douro 2012

★ ★ ★ ★

DOC DOURO $8.95 (239046) **XD**

This is another of the well-priced, hearty reds that Portugal produces. Made from tinta roriz and tinta barroca, as well as touriga franca, this very dry red shows an attractive, young rusticity, and makes you think of grilled spicy sausages and barbecued red meats. The flavours are concentrated and generous, the acidity is properly balanced, the tannins are drying and the texture is tangy and bright.

NOTES

....
....
....
....

Quartetto 2009

★ ★ ★ ★

VINHO REGIONAL ALENTEJANO $10.30   (253880) **D**

With a name like Quartetto, you might think this was a blend of four grape varieties. But no, there are three: aragonez, syrah and alicante bouchet. This trio plays well, giving us a red wine with concentrated flavours, a pleasant tangy and juicy texture and a real dryness from the tannins. Make it a quartet by adding food, something like grilled red meat or spicy sausages.

NOTES

....

....

....

....

SOUTH AFRICA

MOST OF THE WINE REGIONS OF SOUTH AFRICA are warm, and this tends to make for reds that have concentrated flavours and fairly high alcohol. The conditions are right for a wide range of grape varieties. The country's signature red grape is pinotage, a cross of two varieties that was developed there in the 1920s. More popular varieties found in the LCBO are shiraz, merlot and cabernet sauvignon.

Wines from official South African wine regions are called Wines of Origin. In this list, the letters WO followed by a region indicate where the wine is from.

★ ★ ★ ★

The Beachhouse Shiraz/Mourvèdre/Viognier 2013

WO WESTERN CAPE $9.95   (223453)   D

These are three grapes from southern France, and they do well in the warm growing conditions of South Africa. Beachhouse Red is a well-made blend that strikes a great note for its price. It shows well-concentrated, solid and modestly complex fruit and it's nicely balanced, with the fresh acidity contributing tanginess to the texture. Minimally tannic, it makes a good wine for hamburgers and grilled red meats.

NOTES
....
....
....
....

NEW!
★ ★ ★ ★

Big Oak Red 2012

WO WESTERN CAPE $11.80   (350595)

This blend of shiraz and cabernet sauvignon is made by Bellingham, a reliable South African producer. Don't worry, this is not a big, oaky wine; it's named for the tree in the garden of the winery's founders. It's an easy-drinking blend that shows character and some complexity, through and through, and it's a natural for the barbecue circuit.

NOTES
....
....
....
....

NEW!
★ ★ ★ ★ ½

Cathedral Cellar Cabernet Sauvignon 2010

WO WESTERN CAPE $15.95 (328567) XD

[Vintages Essential] This is a quite impressive cabernet sauvignon, packed with plenty of fruit and flavour complexity, with the added assets of structure and balance. The weight of the fruit is offset by judiciously calibrated acidity, making it easy to drink and great with food. It's a natural choice for grilled red meats, whether steak or hamburgers, or anything in between.

NOTES
....
....
....
....
....

Durbanville Hills Shiraz 2011

★ ★ ★ ★

WO DURBANVILLE $11.95   (22269) **XD**

Although Australians grabbed shiraz as their signature wine and made it the big variety success story of the 1990s, they don't have the field entirely to themselves. South Africa produces some notable examples. This one is well made and delivers good fruitiness. It's fairly complex, as well as flavoursome and it has good fruit–acid balance. It goes well with burgers and red meat.

NOTES

....
....
....
....

Goats do Roam Red 2013

★ ★ ★ ★

WO WESTERN CAPE $12.95 (718940) **XD**

The story goes that the winery's goats got into the vineyards and ate the best and tastiest fruit. Sounds like they have a great future as consultants. It's also a play on words for the côtes du Rhône grape varieties (syrah, cinsault, mourvèdre, carignan, grenache) used in the blend. This is consistently well made, vintage after vintage, with defined flavours and excellent balance. Drink it with red meats, pork and poultry.

NOTES

....
....
....
....

Nederburg 'Winemaster's Reserve' Shiraz 2012

★ ★ ★ ★

WO WESTERN CAPE $11.45   (527457) **D**

The striking characteristic of this dry, medium-weight shiraz is its balance. You'll find all the concentrated fruit flavours you expect from the variety but, unlike many at this price that are fruity and flat, the texture here is juicy and refreshing. That means it goes especially well with food, and it's versatile enough to handle red meats, veal, pork and poultry.

NOTES

....
....
....
....

Porcupine Ridge Syrah 2013

★ ★ ★ ★ ½

WO SWARTLAND $14.95 (595280) **XD**

[Vintages Essential] This is an impressive syrah in a distinctly New World style, with plenty of fruit up front, but it carries its weight well and delivers effectively in balance and structure. The dense, dark, spicy flavours are reined in by fresh acidity, and the tannins are drying. This is made for red meat, so drink it with well-seasoned steak or lamb.

NOTES

....

....

....

....

....

The Wolftrap Syrah/Mourvèdre/Viognier 2012

★ ★ ★ ★ ½

WO WESTERN CAPE $13.95 (292557) **D**

Made by prestigious South African producer Boekenhoutskloof, this is a delicious blend that's a natural for grilled, well-seasoned red meats. It's dry and well balanced, with quite rich, dark fruit flavours that show plenty of complexity. The acidity comes through effectively, keeping it fresh, and the tannins are ripe and slightly gripping, but very manageable.

NOTES

....

....

....

....

....

SPAIN

SPAIN IS WELL KNOWN for its red wines. Among the many wine regions, Rioja is probably the most recognizable, but you'll find reds from a number of others on this list. Tempranillo is Spain's signature grape variety, but wine is made from many other native and international varieties, as this selection shows.

The initials DO (*Denominación de Origen*) indicate a wine from one of Spain's designated wine regions. Two of them, Rioja and Priorat, have been elevated to DOC (*Denominación de Origen Calificada*) level.

NEW!
★ ★ ★ ★

Beronia Rioja Tempranillo 2011

DOC RIOJA $12.75 (243055) **XD**

Tempranillo is Spain and Rioja's signature red grape. Here it makes a high-toned wine with bright, concentrated and reasonably complex fruit, underpinned by a seam of clean, fresh acidity. The tannins are drying and moderate. This is a good choice for simple red meat dishes, as well as for roast or grilled pork.

NOTES
....
....
....
....

★ ★ ★ ★

Campo Viejo Rioja Reserva 2008

DOC RIOJA $17.95 (137810) **XD**

Unlike a generic rioja, a rioja reserva has to age for a specified number of years in barrel and bottle before going on sale. For that reason, reservas tend to have more intensity and complexity, as this one does. It delivers quite intense and complex flavours, a rich and tangy texture and good tannic structure. Medium bodied and dry, it goes well with grilled or roasted red meats or with meat cooked in red wine.

NOTES
....
....
....
....

★ ★ ★ ★

Castillo de Almansa Reserva 2010

DO ALMANSA $11.95 (270363) **XD**

Almansa is a small wine region not far inland from Spain's Mediterranean coast, where the days get very hot during the growing season. It shows in this wine, which has concentrated and quite complex flavours of sweet fruit. It's bone dry and medium bodied, with firm tannins and a tangy texture. It goes very nicely with well-seasoned red meat dishes all year round, and with hearty stews in winter.

NOTES
....
....
....
....

★ ★ ★ ★

Castillo de Monséran Garnacha 2011

DO CARIÑENA $9.95   (73395) D

This is a basic red that's well priced and great for drinking on the patio when you're serving burgers, ribs and other well-seasoned red meats. Made from the grape variety better known as grenache, it delivers rich and intense sweet fruit flavours with limited complexity, along with a tangy texture. It's medium bodied and negligibly tannic.

NOTES

....

....

....

....

★ ★ ★ ★ ½

Ebeia Roble 2012

DO RIBERA DEL DUERO $14.95 (307710) D

This tempranillo-based wine stands out for the excellent acid–fruit balance that makes it ideal for food. The fruit is weighty and quite dense, complex and persistent, but the acidity cuts through nicely. The tannins are quite firm but navigable. It's great with paella, grilled spicy sausages and many red meat dishes.

NOTES

....

....

....

....

....

★ ★ ★ ★ ½

Gran Feudo Reserva 2008

DO NAVARRA $16.95 (479014) D

[Vintages Essential] Made from tempranillo, Spain's signature grape variety, and cabernet sauvignon and merlot, this very attractive dry red goes well with all kinds of grilled red meat, as well as hearty stews and risottos whether or not they feature meat. The fruit is ripe and sweet with layered complexity, and it's underpinned by refreshing acidity and framed by moderate tannins.

NOTES

....

....

....

....

Hécula 2011

★ ★ ★ ★ ½

DO YECLA $11.70 (300673) **XD**

This is 100 percent monastrell, which is known under many aliases, including mourvèdre and mataró. Monastrell is the signature grape of Yecla, and this version is quite a big and dense red, with rich, layered flavours tempered by fresh acidity. Dry and lightly tannic, this very well-made wine is a natural for hearty risottos, red meats and stews.

NOTES

....

....

....

....

Hoya de Cadenas Reserva Tempranillo 2009

★ ★ ★ ★

DO UTIEL-REQUENA $12.55 (620989) **XD**

The appellation is little known (it's near Valencia), but the grape variety is famous; it's Spain's signature and the basis for wines from Rioja. Here it's made in a straightforward, uncomplicated style, with plenty of solid fruit that's consistent from start to finish. It's nicely integrated with the acidity and has a tangy texture that pairs well with pork, veal, rich pasta dishes and many risottos.

NOTES

....

....

....

....

Las Rocas de San Alejandro Garnacha 2011

★ ★ ★ ★

DO CALATAYUD $16.75 (269977) **D**

This is made 100 percent from 80-year-old garnacha (alias grenache). It's said that older vines, with their low fruit yield, produce grapes with more concentration and complexity, and you can taste and feel it here. This is intensely flavoured and solid right through the palate, and it has the added assets of complexity, balance and (for drinking now) soft tannins. Enjoy it with red meats and hearty casseroles.

NOTES

....

....

....

....

....

Marqués de Riscal Reserva Rioja 2008

★ ★ ★ ★ ½

DOC RIOJA $25.75   (32656) XD

Made mainly from the tempranillo variety, with assistance from graciano and mazuelo, this is aged more than two years in oak barrels and a number more in the bottle before you can buy it. It's one of the older vintages in the LCBO, and it shows ripe, bright and maturing flavours with fresh acidity and moderate, drying tannins. It's a good choice for paella, red meats, pork and many older, full-flavoured cheeses.

NOTES
....
....
....
....

Montecillo Reserva Rioja 2008

★ ★ ★ ★ ½

DOC RIOJA $18.95 (621003) XD

This is a lovely example of a reserva rioja—aged for a minimum time in barrel and bottle and not sold until four years after vintage. Look for elegance across the board here, with concentrated and layered flavours, very good balance and a smooth, attractive texture. Drink it with red meats, well-seasoned poultry or aged, full-flavour cheeses such as manchego.

NOTES
....
....
....
....

Muga Reserva Rioja 2009

★ ★ ★ ★ ★

DOC RIOJA $23.95 (177345) XD

[Vintages Essential] Muga is an iconic name in Spanish wine, and this rioja is tremendous value. It's a blend of tempranillo (70 percent), grenache (20 percent), mazuelo (7 percent) and graciano (3 percent), and it delivers wonderful flavour concentration and complexity. It's very dry and moderately tannic, yet light on its feet, and it has the tanginess that suits food. Drink it with grilled red meats and hearty stews.

NOTES
....
....
....
....

Torres 'Gran Coronas' Reserva Cabernet Sauvignon 2010

★ ★ ★ ★ ★

DO PENEDÈS $19.00   (36483)   **D**

[Vintages Essential] Torres is one of the best-known names in Spanish wine, and this cabernet sauvignon (with 15 percent tempranillo blended in to give it some Spanish blood) shows the quality and value that underlie its reputation. The fruit is sweet, ripe, layered and concentrated, and the texture is generous and tangy. It's medium to full in body and dry, and it has a good tannic grip. Enjoy it with grilled or braised red meats.

NOTES

....

....

....

....

Torres Infinite 2011

★ ★ ★ ★

DO CATALUNYA $12.95   (231795)   **D**

Mostly (85 percent) tempranillo, with the rest cabernet sauvignon, this is an attractive red that goes well with red meats, pork, rich poultry (like coq au vin) and many paellas. It's quite rich and smooth textured, with concentrated flavours that are consistent right through the palate. Dry and medium weight, it shows very manageable and drying tannins.

NOTES

....

....

....

....

....

RED WINES

WASHINGTON

WASHINGTON STATE IS WELL KNOWN for its reds, particularly merlot from the Columbia Valley region. Like other US states, with the obvious exception of California, it is seldom represented on the LCBO's shelves.

★ ★ ★ ★

14 Hands 'Hot to Trot' Red Blend 2011

WASHINGTON STATE $16.70   (226522) **D**

Named for the wild horses that used to live in the hills of Washington
State, this blend brings together merlot, syrah and cabernet sauvignon,
with a dash of mourvèdre and some other red varieties. It's intensely
flavoured with good layered complexity, and it has a nice seam of clean
acidity to keep the fruit honest. It's a very good choice for red meats, as
well as burgers and ribs.

NOTES
....
....
....
....

NEW!
★ ★ ★ ★

Charles & Charles 'Post No. 35'
Cabernet Sauvignon & Syrah 2012

COLUMBIA VALLEY $16.95   (363838)

This is a big-bodied blend that's 58 percent cabernet and 42 percent syrah.
Both varieties are represented well in the flavours, which are concentrated,
deep and well layered, and which hold true from start to long finish. The
acidity is balanced and the tannins are easygoing. This is a hefty wine that
calls for hefty food, so bring it along when eating a plate of grilled red
meat, ribs or well-seasoned sausages.

NOTES
....
....
....
....

ROSÉS

ROSÉ WINE HAS ENJOYED A RENAISSANCE in the last couple of years. Until recently, too many were sweet and simple—fine for everyday drinking but not particularly complex or interesting. Things have changed and rosé has become a popular style, leading producers to make more and more that are well balanced and structured. There are more dry rosés now, along with well-made sweeter styles, and producers have begun to show the varieties, just as they do for whites and reds.

Beginning in spring, the LCBO releases a large number of rosés for the warm months, when demand is highest. But rosés make good drinking all year round.

Cave Spring Rosé 2012

★ ★ ★ ★

VQA NIAGARA ESCARPMENT $14.95 (295006) **XD**

Today many winemakers are trying to make "serious" rosés, and too often these wines are reds in all but colour. Taste them blind and you'd think you were drinking red wine. This cabernet franc rosé is in a more familiar style, with vibrant, fresh, fruity flavours. It's dry and medium weight, with a crisp, clean texture. It goes well with roast ham or turkey, or summer salads.

NOTES

....

....

....

....

Gran Feudo Rosado 2012

★ ★ ★ ★

DO NAVARRA $11.95 (165845) **XD**

This rosé is made mainly from the garnacha tinta (black grenache) variety. After the grapes are pressed, the juice is left on the skins for 24 hours, just long enough for them to make the juice a bright pink colour. Apart from the hue, the texture and flavours are also attractive. It's a mid-weight, dry, well-balanced rosé, with good concentration and focus, and it goes well— all year round—with white fish and many poultry dishes.

NOTES

....

....

....

....

NEW!

Henry of Pelham Rosé 2013

★ ★ ★ ★

VQA NIAGARA PENINSULA $13.95 (613471) **D**

Dry and vibrantly fruity, this electric-pink rosé draws on half a dozen varieties (including zweigelt, pinot noir and cabernet sauvignon) that change each year. It's well balanced and a fairly substantial rosé that you can drink on its own or pair successfully with roast or grilled chicken and pork.

NOTES

....

....

....

....

....

Malivoire 'LadyBug' Rosé 2012

★ ★ ★ ★ ½

VQA NIAGARA PENINSULA $15.95   (559088)   **D**

[Vintages Essential] Malivoire's LadyBug rosé, a blend of cabernet franc, gamay and pinot noir, has been a hit for more than ten years. One of the earliest of a new generation of rosés, it's dry and full bodied, but it's definitively a rosé, not a red in pink clothing. Look for a great fruit–acid balance, and enjoy this with baked ham or roast poultry.

NOTES

....

....

....

....

Ogier Ventoux Rosé 2012

★ ★ ★ ★

AOC VENTOUX $11.75   (134916)   **XD**

A blend of grenache, syrah and cinsault from the South of France, this is a dry rosé that drinks well on its own and pairs well with summer salads and roast chicken. Look for bright and nicely concentrated flavours paired with good acidity that translates to a crisp, clean texture.

NOTES

....

....

....

....

SPARKLING WINES
& CHAMPAGNES

HERE'S THE DIFFERENCE BETWEEN CHAMPAGNE and sparkling wine: All champagnes are sparkling wines, but not all sparkling wines are champagnes. Champagne is a sparkling wine made in the Champagne region of France from specified grape varieties and in a method defined by wine law. Sparkling wines made elsewhere (even if from the same grape varieties and in the same method) cannot be called champagne.

In this section, the sparkling wines are reviewed first, followed by the champagnes.

In line with changing tastes, more and more restaurants offer sparkling wine by the glass, to drink either as an aperitif or with meals. Dry sparkling wine goes well with many dishes, such as fish, seafood, poultry and pork. Fruitier or off-dry styles are excellent with spicy dishes, such as much Asian cuisine, with which you might otherwise drink beer.

Sparkling wine has been made for centuries, but there's no clear answer to the question of where or when it was made first. A credible claim comes from Limoux, in southwest France, where it seems to have been made in the 1500s and where a sparkling wine called Blanquette de Limoux is now made. Sparkling wine was popularized by producers in France's Champagne region, where sparkling wine was first made in the late 1600s by a monk called Dom Pérignon.

Much of the Dom Pérignon story is myth, but there's no doubt about the success of champagne. It was aggressively marketed in the 1800s and became associated with special events of all kinds. Generations later, champagne continues to feature at celebrations as varied as ship launchings, Grand Prix victories and weddings.

But although it has become the brand name for sparkling wine, only some sparkling wine is genuine champagne. To be labelled as such, the wine has to be made using specific grape varieties from vineyards in the Champagne region of northeast France according to a specific method. That method involves adding sugar and alcohol to base wine and allowing a second fermentation to occur in the bottle that is sold to the consumer. This procedure is known variously as the champagne method, traditional method or classic method (and their French translations).

Even when they use the specified grape varieties and employ the champagne method, producers elsewhere are not permitted to label their wines "champagne." In fact, they can't describe the wine as being made by the champagne method and must use an alternative term. Sparkling wine can be produced using other methods, too, and many (but not all) of the less expensive sparkling wines are made using techniques that are less costly and time-consuming. One involves a second fermentation in a tank, with the sparkling wine being bottled under pressure. Another involves carbonating wine in the same way as soft drinks.

Apart from champagne, there are several other common categories of sparkling wine: cava, prosecco and crémant.

- CAVA (which means "cellar") is made in the northeast of Spain according to the same method used to make champagne, but generally using grape varieties native to Spain.
- PROSECCO is an Italian sparkling wine made from the glera grape variety. It tends to be fruitier than cava and champagne.
- CRÉMANT is a category of wines from French regions, such as Crémant de Bourgogne and Crémant de Loire, made according to the same method used to make champagne.

Some other terms you find on labels of sparkling wine refer to dryness, which is based on the amount of residual sugar in the wine. Most sparkling wines are labelled "brut," which means they taste dry. "Extra brut" means they are even drier, while wines labelled "sec" are a little sweeter.

Unlike most still wines, sparkling wines are generally non-vintage and don't show a year on their label. This is because the base wine used to make sparkling wine is usually drawn from several vintages. Vintage-dated sparkling wines do exist, but they tend to be more expensive, especially vintage champagne.

A WORD OF CAUTION: Sparkling wine is under pressure, and you should take care not to let the cork shoot out of the bottle; it can seriously injure you or someone else. Always keep your thumb on the cork as you remove the foil and wire cage. Open the bottle by holding the cork and twisting the bottle, not vice versa. You can also hold a cloth, like a tea towel, over the cork to make sure it doesn't escape. Ease the cork from the bottle so that you hear a gentle hiss, rather than a loud pop.

The following list of best-value sparkling wines carried by the LCBO is divided into two categories: sparkling wines and champagnes.

SPARKLING WINES

★ ★ ★ ★   **Astoria Prosecco**

DOC PROSECCO, ITALY $13.90   (593855)   **D**

[Non-vintage] Although many people think prosecco is a style of wine, it's a grape variety used to make sparkling wine in the northeastern corner of Italy. (It has been renamed "glera.") It tends to be off-dry, like this example, which is fruity and easy drinking. It's ideal for sipping before a meal, but you can also serve it with spicy food, as the sparkling fruitiness will help tone down the heat.

NOTES

....

....

....

NEW!
★ ★ ★ ★   **Bottega 'Il Vino dei Poeti' Rosé Brut Sparkling Wine**

ITALY $13.45   (277202)

This is a very attractive, dry sparkling wine that is very good to sip on its own or to drink with lighter foods. It goes well with prosciutto and melon. The flavours are bright and fresh, the acidity is crisp and balanced and there are ample fine bubbles. It's a very affordable sparkling rosé for celebrations.

NOTES

....

....

....

★ ★ ★ ★ ½   **Cave Spring 'Blanc de Blancs' Brut Sparkling Wine**

VQA NIAGARA ESCARPMENT, ONTARIO $29.95   (213983)   **D**

This lovely bottle of bubbles was made from chardonnay grapes (hence the reference to white grapes in 'Blanc de Blancs') in the traditional method used to make champagne. It shows stylish fruit that's defined and focused, supported by well-calibrated acidity and enhanced by the streams of fine bubbles. It's fine drinking on its own or with seafood, shellfish, fish, poultry and pork.

NOTES

....

....

....

★ ★ ★ ★ Château de Montgueret Brut Crémant de Loire

AOC CRÉMANT DE LOIRE, FRANCE $19.95 (217760) **XD**

[Non-vintage] This sparkling wine from the Loire Valley is made the same way as champagne. It's a lovely blend of chenin blanc, chardonnay and cabernet franc. Slightly off-dry with attractive and complex flavours, it's an excellent aperitif that will perk up your appetite. Or pair it with spicy Asian dishes, especially seafood like garlic and ginger shrimp.

NOTES

....

....

....

....

★ ★ ★ ★ ½ Château des Charmes Brut Sparkling Wine

VQA NIAGARA-ON-THE-LAKE, ONTARIO $22.95 (224766) **XD**

[Non-vintage] Made from chardonnay and pinot noir and in the traditional method developed in Champagne, this is a lovely dry sparkling wine that delivers quality from start to finish. The flavours are pungent and nuanced with good concentration, and the acidity is bright and correct. There are plenty of bubbles, contributing to a finely-grained, crisp mousse. Drink it alone or with poultry, pork, white fish, seafood or smoked salmon.

NOTES

....

....

....

....

★ ★ ★ ★ ★ Codorníu Brut Clasico Cava

DO CAVA, SPAIN $12.90 (215814) **XD**

[Non-vintage] Cava is made in the same way as champagne, which is to say that it goes through fermentation in the actual bottle you buy (rather than being bottled after the fermentation is complete). This is a very attractive example, with great flavours and a lovely crisp and balanced texture. It has plenty of small bubbles and a soft mousse. Sip it alone or serve it with spicy chicken, pork or seafood.

NOTES

....

....

....

....

★ ★ ★ ★

Cono Sur Brut Sparkling Wine

DO BIO-BIO VALLEY, CHILE $13.95   (215079) **D**

[Non-vintage] There's a touch of sweetness in this, but just enough to make it easy drinking. From one of the most southerly wine regions in Chile, this has good balance, good fruit all through the palate, a crisp texture and plenty of bubbles that produce a foamy mousse. You can drink this on its own or with slightly spicy seafood and chicken dishes.

NOTES

....

....

....

....

NEW!
★ ★ ★ ★ ½

Cuvée 13 Rosé Sparkling Wine

VQA NIAGARA PENINSULA, ONTARIO $24.95   (147504) **D**

[Vintages Essential] Made from pinot noir and chardonnay, using the method employed in Champagne, this is a lovely sparkling rosé that is very versatile at the table. You can drink it on its own or pair it with fish, seafood, poultry and pork. It's dry, crisp and clean, with well-calibrated fruit and balanced acidity, bright and serious fruit flavours and plenty of fine bubbles.

NOTES

....

....

....

....

....

★ ★ ★ ★ ½

De Chanceny Brut Rosé Crémant de Loire

AOC CRÉMANT DE LOIRE, FRANCE $19.35   (211466) **D**

[Non-vintage] "Crémant" indicates a sparkling wine from a number of French wine regions. This one, a rosé, is from the Loire Valley, where it's made from cabernet franc, and shows lively fruit flavours. The texture is crisp and clean and the bubbles are plentiful. This makes a fine sparkler to drink on its own, and goes well with roast turkey and cranberries.

NOTES

....

....

....

....

....

★ ★ ★ ★

Freixenet 'Cordon Negro' Brut Cava

DO CAVA, SPAIN $13.95   (216945) **D**

[Non-vintage] This is one of those reliable, versatile sparkling wines that you can count on, batch after batch. A blend of three grape varieties indigenous to Spain and made in the same way as champagne (it was fermented in the bottle you buy), it delivers lovely vibrant fruit flavours and has a zesty and refreshing texture. It has all the fizz you want for a special occasion, for an aperitif or for a spicy Asian dish.

NOTES
....
....
....
....

★ ★ ★ ★

Freixenet 'Cordon Rosado' Brut Cava

DO CAVA, SPAIN $13.95   (217059) **D**

[Non-vintage] This is a rosé sparkling wine that makes a pretty addition to a summer table—or is a reminder on a winter table that summer will eventually return. It has bright, ripe, sweet fruit flavours, but the wine itself is bone dry. The texture is crisp and refreshing and the bubbles are plentiful and create a lovely mousse. This is perfect with a summer salad, but you can also serve it with baked ham or roast chicken.

NOTES
....
....
....

★ ★ ★ ★ ½

Henry of Pelham 'Cuvée Catharine' Brut Rosé Sparkling Wine

VQA NIAGARA PENINSULA, ONTARIO $29.95 (217505) **XD**

[Non-vintage] This is a lovely sparkling rosé made from chardonnay and pinot noir by the method used in Champagne (although the winemaker is not permitted to express it that way on the label). You'll find very attractive vibrant fruit flavours here, echoed by the crisp, refreshing texture and fine bubbles. This is a lovely wine for the summer (or winter) table, and it's great for roast turkey, salads and spicy dishes featuring chicken and seafood.

NOTES
....
....

....

Henry of Pelham 'Cuvée Catharine' Brut Sparkling Wine

★ ★ ★ ★ ½ VQA NIAGARA PENINSULA, ONTARIO $29.95 (217521) **XD**

[Non-vintage] Made from chardonnay and pinot noir, the two varieties most often used in champagne, this sparkling wine is dry, crisp and compelling. The flavours are layered and defined, with a complex profile, and they're lifted by the vibrant acidity and steady streams of fine bubbles. The mousse is clean and crisp, and this is great with oysters, shellfish and seafood in general, or as a partner to pork or white fish.

NOTES

....

....

....

....

Hungaria 'Grande Cuvée' Brut Sparkling Wine

★ ★ ★ ★   HUNGARY $12.25   (619288) **D**

[Non-vintage] A very affordable sparkling wine, this is excellent on its own, as an aperitif or with chicken, pork or seafood—or use it as a base for mimosas or cocktails. It has solid, vibrant flavours, plenty of fizz and a moderate, soft mousse. It's dry and the texture is crisp and clean.

NOTES

....

....

....

....

Mionetto Prosecco

★ ★ ★ ★ ½ DOC TREVISO, ITALY $18.85   (266023) **D**

[Non-vintage] This is a quite elegant sparkling wine from the Treviso region near Venice. The flavours are very attractive—bright, vibrant, focused and well defined—and the crisp acidity lightens them without undermining their intensity. There's a good level of fizz and a firm, soft mousse. It's great on its own, as an aperitif or with many pork, poultry and seafood dishes.

NOTES

....

....

....

....

Mumm Cuvée Napa 'Brut Prestige' Sparkling Wine

★ ★ ★ ★

NAPA VALLEY, CALIFORNIA $23.95 (217273) D

[Non-vintage] French fizz tradition comes to California in this sparkling wine made in Napa (using the same grape varieties—pinot noir, chardonnay and pinot meunier—as in champagne) by a famous champagne house. This is a great sparkling wine to drink as an aperitif—it has the crisp, mouth-watering texture that sets you up for food—or enjoy with oysters. The flavours are complex and nuanced and the mousse is soft and defined.

NOTES

....

....

....

Paul Delane Réserve Brut Crémant de Bourgogne

★ ★ ★ ★

AOC CRÉMANT DE BOURGOGNE, FRANCE $21.20 (214981) D

[Non-vintage] This nicely balanced sparkling wine is made from four of Burgundy's permitted varieties: pinot noir, gamay, chardonnay and aligoté. It has a crisp and clean texture from the bright acidity, concentrated flavours and streams of bubbles that end in a good mousse. Sip it on its own or drink it with grilled seafood, smoked salmon or many spicy Asian dishes.

NOTES

....

....

....

....

Santa Margherita Valdobbiadene Superiore Brut Prosecco

★ ★ ★ ★ ½

DOCG VALDOBBIADENE PROSECCO SUPERIORE, ITALY

$17.95 (687582) XD

[Non-vintage] [Vintages Essential] Made in a brut (dry) style, this prosecco is a cut above many of its kind. It has the fruit richness of many proseccos, but it's a lot drier than most and shows more structure and complexity. You can drink this on its own, as an aperitif or paired with a broad spectrum of foods, from seafood, fish and poultry, to pork and spicy Asian dishes.

NOTES

....

....

....

★ ★ ★ ★

Segura Viudas Brut Reserva Cava

DO CAVA, SPAIN $14.25 (216960) **D**

[Non-vintage] Made with the same method as champagne but from different grape varieties, this sparkling wine offers lovely, concentrated flavours and brisk acidity. You'll find streams of bubbles and a soft, attractive mousse. Like many dry sparkling wines, it's extremely versatile on the table; you can pair it with poultry, seafood, fish and spicy dishes (like many curries). Or serve it off the table as a wine to sip on its own.

NOTES

....

....

....

....

NEW!
★ ★ ★ ★

Trapiche Extra Brut Sparkling Wine 2013

MENDOZA, ARGENTINA $11.95 (262261) **D**

Made from chardonnay, semillon and malbec grapes, this sparkling wine is dry with very attractive fruit flavours and is, for its price, nicely structured and complex. The acidity is crisp and clean, giving the wine fresh brightness, and there are plenty of quite fine bubbles. You can drink this on its own, or pair it with fish, seafood, pork or poultry. It's also inexpensive and good enough to use in cocktails.

NOTES

....

....

....

....

CHAMPAGNES

NEW!
★ ★ ★ ★ ½

Cattier 'Premier Cru' Brut Champagne

AOC CHAMPAGNE $42.95 (325720) **XD**

The reference to 'Premier Cru' here refers to the classification of vineyards in Champagne, where the top tier are 'Grand Cru' and the next tier are designated 'Premier Cru.' This champagne shows its pedigree with a clean, elegant texture that supports well-defined and focused flavours. Look for beads of fine bubbles and a generous mousse, and pair it with fish, seafood, poultry or pork.

NOTES

....

....

....

NEW!
★ ★ ★ ★ ★

Louis Roederer 'Brut Premier' Champagne

AOC CHAMPAGNE $68.95 (268771) **XD**

This is a fine champagne that speaks quality and elegance from start to finish. The flavours are well defined and focused, with good complexity and structure. They're more than ably supported by a broad seam of crisp, fresh acidity. The bubbles are fine, the beads are persistent and the mousse is firm and generous. It's a champagne for the table, where it goes well with fish, seafood, pork and poultry.

NOTES

....

....

....

....

★ ★ ★ ★

Mumm 'Carte Classique' Extra Dry Champagne

AOC CHAMPAGNE $61.25 (308064) **D**

[Non-vintage] In the crazy language of wine, extra dry is not as dry as brut. It's sort of middling dry—distinct from very dry—and many people prefer the softer texture of extra dry when they're looking for a champagne to drink on its own. This is a very good choice. It presents lovely fruit flavours, good, clean acidity and a soft but defined mousse. And, of course, you can pair it with food, too!

NOTES

....

....

....

★ ★ ★ ★

Mumm 'Cordon Rouge' Brut Champagne

AOC CHAMPAGNE $61.25 (308056) **XD**

[Non-vintage] You could serve this on Mother's Day, but the Mumm here is pronounced moom, as in "moon." It's one of the best-known champagnes and you can't miss its diagonal red stripe (the "cordon rouge") on the shelf in the LCBO. It's just well made, with all the crispness you want from champagne, not to mention the nuanced flavours. With a soft mousse and good weight, it goes well with chicken, turkey or rich fish dishes.

NOTES

....
....
....
....

★ ★ ★ ★ ½

Nicolas Feuillatte 'Réserve Particulière' Brut Rosé Champagne

AOC CHAMPAGNE $57.95 (267039) **XD**

[Non-vintage] Rosé champagnes are on a roll, with more and more champagne houses producing pink versions of their classics. This one shows bright, vibrant fruit flavours, zesty acidity, plenty of fine bubbles and a soft mousse. The colour, which is more salmon-bronze than pink, adds to your table, and the wine is delicious on its own or with dishes like melon and prosciutto and sautéed shrimp.

NOTES

....
....
....

★ ★ ★ ★ ½

Perrier-Jouët 'Grand Brut' Brut Champagne

AOC CHAMPAGNE $65.95 (155341) **XD**

[Non-vintage] This is a really lovely champagne that sizzles on its own or in the company of food. The flavours are rich, tiered and well focused, and the texture is crisp and elegant. Here you find a winning tension between the brisk acidity and the roundness of the fruit, with hints of lees (dead yeast cells) flickering between. This is a fine aperitif, and it goes well with many seafood, fish, poultry and pork dishes.

NOTES

....
....
....

Piper-Heidsieck Brut Champagne

★ ★ ★ ★ ½

AOC CHAMPAGNE $54.95 (462432) **D**

[Non-vintage] This is a versatile champagne. You can pop the cork (not literally—always ease the cork from a bottle of sparkling wine so that it opens with a gentle hiss, not a pop) to celebrate birthdays and the like, or serve it with chicken, turkey or pork. Dry and medium bodied with solid, complex flavours and a refreshing texture, it shows fine streams of bubbles that make for a clean, crisp mousse.

NOTES

....
....
....
....

Pol Roger 'Extra Cuvée de Réserve' Brut Champagne

★ ★ ★ ★ ½

AOC CHAMPAGNE $61.30 (217158) **XD**

[Non-vintage] This is a very good-quality champagne at a very good price. It has everything you look for in the animal: solid fruit flavours, complexity, a crisp and zesty texture, lots of fine bubbles streaming up from the bottom of the glass and an edgy but quite soft mousse in the mouth. It's ideal as an aperitif, but you can take it to the table and drink it with Asian cuisine or seafood, fish, poultry and pork dishes.

NOTES

....
....
....
....

Taittinger 'Brut Réserve' Champagne

NEW!
★ ★ ★ ★

AOC CHAMPAGNE $58.95 (365312) **XD**

Taittinger is a well-known champagne house, and for good reason. Try this example, and you'll find it quite elegant in style, with well-defined and focused fruit flavours and a crisp, zesty texture emanating from the supporting acidity. Small bubbles stream in fine beads, and the mousse is both firm and yielding. This is a very good champagne for food, and it goes well with many fish, seafood and poultry dishes.

NOTES

....
....
....
....

★ ★ ★ ★ ½

Tarlant 'Brut Réserve' Champagne

AOC CHAMPAGNE $41.90   (325167)   **D**

[Non-vintage] This is a quality champagne priced so that you can drink it on occasions that are special simply because you have a bottle and feel like opening it. It's for sipping on its (and your) own on a "champagne Sunday," or taking to the table for poultry or pork dishes. In any event, it's long on flavours and complexity, with crisp freshness, fine bubbles and a generous mousse.

NOTES

....

....

....

....

★ ★ ★ ★

Veuve Clicquot Ponsardin Brut Champagne

AOC CHAMPAGNE $67.95 (563338) **XD**

[Non-vintage] Named for the woman who not only took over production but improved it after her champagne-producer husband died, this has become an iconic champagne whose stylish yellow-orange label stands out on the shelf. The champagne itself is a byword for balance, with well-defined flavours, a crisp, refreshing texture and fine bubbles and mousse. You can drink this on its own or with smoked salmon, chicken or pork.

NOTES

....

....

....

....

★ ★ ★ ★ ½

Victoire 'Prestige' Brut Champagne

AOC CHAMPAGNE $39.95   (190025)   **D**

[Non-vintage] This is a very good price for the quality. The texture is crisp and bright, with good complexity and yeast notes, and the flavours are nicely layered and consistent right through the palate. It throws plenty of fine bubbles, forms a firm but gentle mousse and is great sipped on its own, as an aperitif or with white meats and fish.

NOTES

....

....

....

....

....

SWEET &
DESSERT WINES

ALL DESSERT WINES ARE SWEET, but not all sweet wines are suitable for dessert. For example, icewine, which is a style Ontario is famous for, is often too sweet for desserts but goes well with foie gras (which is normally served as an appetizer or part of a main course) and blue cheese. This list includes a number of sweet wines, and I've suggested what goes best with each.

★ ★ ★ ★

Batasiolo 'Bosc dla Rei' Moscato d'Asti 2012

DOCG MOSCATO D'ASTI, ITALY $14.95   (277194) **S**

Made from the moscato variety, this is a luscious, moderately sweet wine that goes well with cheesecakes and fruit pies. It has a round texture allied to good acidity, and is very lightly viscous. It would also go well with foie gras or a cheese course that included not-too-strong blue cheeses.

NOTES

....

....

....

....

★ ★ ★ ★ ½

Cave Spring 'Indian Summer' Select Late Harvest Riesling 2011

VQA NIAGARA PENINSULA, ONTARIO $24.95   (415901) **S**

[Vintages Essential, 375 mL] This is not icewine, although the grapes were partly frozen when picked. They were left on the vine past the usual harvest date to shrivel and lose water, then picked after the first frost. The result is a wine with sweet—but not very sweet—flavours that are complex and delicious, complemented by vibrant acidity. It's lovely to drink by itself, but you can serve it (chilled) with any fruit-based dessert that's no sweeter than the wine.

NOTES

....

....

....

....

NEW!
★ ★ ★ ★ ★

Domaine Pinnacle Cidre de Glace/Ice Cider

QUEBEC $24.95   (94094) **S**

[375mL] This is one of two fruit wines (not made from grapes) in this book, and it's a beauty. Ice cider is made in a way similar to icewine, by freezing the fruit to separate its water from the juice. The result here is a rich, sweet, slightly viscous wine that has distinct apple and some honeyed flavours. Just as important, it has the bright acidity to keep the sweetness in check. Drink it with not-too-sweet fruit (especially apple) desserts.

NOTES

....

....

....

....

Henry of Pelham Riesling Icewine 2012

★ ★ ★ ★ ★

VQA SHORT HILLS BENCH, ONTARIO $49.95   (430561)   S

[Vintages Essential, 375 mL] This is an icewine that delivers the best in the style. It has all the sweetness that shrivelled and frozen grapes can produce, but it's nuanced and layered. Meanwhile, the threat of a cloying, teeth-hurting experience is averted by the nice line of acidity. It's a more drinkable icewine than many, and for this reason you could chill it slightly (about 15 minutes in the fridge), then sip it by itself or drink it with foie gras or briny blue cheese.

NOTES

....

....

....

Henry of Pelham Special Select Late Harvest Vidal 2012

★ ★ ★ ★ ½

VQA ONTARIO $19.95   (395228)   S

This stylish wine is made from selected vidal grapes from bunches left on the vines well after the normal harvest period. With concentrated sugar, they have produced a luscious wine that goes well with sweet, fruit-based desserts, briny blue cheese or seared foie gras. The dense and focused sweet flavours are balanced by brisk and vibrant acidity that cuts through the sweetness and ensures it's not cloying.

NOTES

....

....

....

....

Inniskillin Vidal Icewine 2012

★ ★ ★ ★

VQA NIAGARA PENINSULA, ONTARIO $49.95   (551085)   S

[Vintages Essential] Inniskillin is arguably the world's best-known icewine producer. They make icewine from a number of grape varieties, and this vidal version delivers all the rich, pungent sweetness you buy icewine for, effectively offset by a seam of vibrant acidity. It gives the wine a sort of juiciness that enables you to enjoy it on its own, with blue cheese or with foie gras.

NOTES

....

....

....

....

Ironstone 'Obsession' Symphony 2012

★ ★ ★ ★

CALIFORNIA $15.20 (295931) **M**

This is a sweet (but not too sweet) wine made from the symphony variety,
an aromatic cross of muscat of Alexandria and grenache gris. The flavours
are intense and pungent, but a good dose of acidity takes care of much of
the sweetness. (Think of a fairly rich gewürztraminer.) Chilled to bring
out the acidity, this is a good partner for many spicy Asian dishes.

NOTES

....

....

....

....

....

Southbrook Framboise

★ ★ ★ ★ ½

ONTARIO $15.95   (341024) **S**

[Non-vintage, 375 mL] This is one of two fruit wines (non-grape wine)
in this book. Southbrook's framboise, made from the royalty variety of
raspberries and fortified with a little brandy, has become an icon, so it's
here. It's full of rich, intense, sweet flavours, and the viscous texture has
the acidity to cut through the sweetness. Drink it with rich chocolate
desserts or pour it over ice cream. Amazing!

NOTES

....

....

....

....

FORTIFIED WINES

FORTIFIED WINES ARE WINES whose alcohol level has been raised, and style modified, by the addition of brandy or a neutral, distilled alcohol. The best-known fortified wines are port and sherry.

Port is a sweet, fortified wine (usually red, sometimes white) made in the Douro region of Portugal. It's generally served after dinner with dessert, cheese or nuts, or on its own, and some people like the combination of port and a cigar. Port can also be served as an aperitif, a common practice in France. Although other countries produce fortified wines labelled "port," the name is properly reserved for the wine produced in the Douro region according to the rules set out for port production there.

Sherry is a fortified wine made in Jerez, a wine region in the south of Spain. It comes in many styles, from clear, crisp, light and dry to black, heavy, viscous and sweet. You'll find other fortified wines labelled sherry, but only fortified wine from the Jerez region made in a designated way can properly be called sherry. Although sherry is fortified and is generally drunk as an aperitif, it is also a very successful partner for food, and the spectrum of styles is broad enough that it's possible to find a sherry for any dish.

Ferreira 'Dona Antonia Reserve' Porto

★ ★ ★ ★ ½

DOC PORTO $18.95   (157586) S

Named for the head of the Ferreira port-producing family from the early nineteenth century, this is a luscious port. It delivers sweet, rich, multi-layered flavours and a texture that's quite viscous and seems to swell in your mouth. But the acidity clicks in and kills the sweetness, leaving you with a fruity and complex finish. It's delicious on its own or with blue cheese and roasted nuts.

NOTES

....
....
....

Graham's 10-Year Tawny Port

★ ★ ★ ★ ½

DOC PORTO $27.95 (206508) MS

This is a luscious tawny port, so called for the golden-brown colour it achieves from oxidation and being stored in barrels. This is medium on the sweetness scale, with loads of complexity in the flavour profile. It's a little viscous, has good acid balance and drinks well on its own. If you prefer, you can drink it with bitter chocolate or briny blue cheeses.

NOTES

....
....
....
....

Graham's 20-Year Tawny Port

★ ★ ★ ★ ½

DOC PORTO $36.95   (620641) S

[500 mL] To be labelled as "10-year" or "20-year," ports don't need to spend that long in oak barrels; they need to achieve the quality and style a port typically would if it did. But these ports do have long aging, and this one shows it in its structure and the complexity and depth of its flavours. It's elegant, smooth and best appreciated on its own, at least for the first few sips. Then bring on the Stilton cheese.

NOTES

....
....
....
....

Quinta do Noval Tawny Port

NEW!
★ ★ ★ ★

DOC PORTO $17.70   (309765) **S**

As "tawny" suggests, this is bright, mid-range amber in colour. The flavours are rich and sweet, and it has some viscosity in the texture. The acidity is good, though, and the sweetness is anything but cloying. You can drink this on its own (some people prefer it slightly chilled) or with desserts, such as stewed fruits.

NOTES

....

....

....

....

....

Sandeman Late Bottled Vintage Port 2009

★ ★ ★ ★

DOC PORTO $16.95   (195974) **S**

True to its name, this port from the 2009 vintage was bottled in 2013. It's a classic LBV, with depth and intensity of flavour and texture. Lightly viscous, it shows plenty of complexity as it moves through the palate, and is well balanced and nicely tannic. Port is one of the rare wines that go with chocolate (dark and bitter), so indulge!

NOTES

....

....

....

....

Taylor Fladgate 'First Estate' Reserve Port

★ ★ ★ ★ ½

DOC PORTO $16.55   (309401) **S**

This is made in a slightly less-sweet style than most ports. There are some red wines described as port-like because they're so rich, intense and sweet, and if you think of those, this port is just across the line, in a style approaching red wine. Being less sweet, it's easier drinking and goes well with aged cheeses (like very old, crumbly cheddar). The texture here is intense and rich, but it leaves a drying sensation in your mouth.

NOTES

....

....

....

....

....

Warre's 'Otima' 10-Year Port

★ ★ ★ ★

DOC PORTO $22.95 (566174) S

[500 mL] If you think of port as an after-dinner drink with the colour and weight of the leather armchairs of the crusty old guys who drink it, try Otima. It's made in a lighter style—as you might expect from the colour of this port, which is paler than most—but it still has lovely sweet fruit flavours. You can chill it as an aperitif or drink it at room temperature after dinner.

NOTES

....

....

....

....

SHERRIES

★ ★ ★ ★

Alvear's Fino Montilla

DOC MONTILLA-MORILES $12.10 (112771) **XD**

[Non-vintage] This isn't sherry, as it isn't made in Jerez, in southern Spain. Montilla, the region next to Jerez, produces wines in the same styles as sherry, from delicate and bone dry to rich and sweet. This one is on the delicate and dry end of the spectrum. It's crisp and refreshing, with a light body, and it goes well with salty Spanish tapas like olives and grilled octopus.

NOTES

....

....

....

....

★ ★ ★ ★ ½

Tio Pepe Extra Dry Fino Sherry

DO JEREZ $16.40 (231829) **XD**

[Non-vintage] Tio Pepe is an iconic fino sherry. Made in an astringently dry style ("extra dry" isn't an exaggeration!), it has pungent, high-toned flavours backed by high, taut acidity. It's not to everyone's taste when drunk on its own, but it's an excellent partner for many Spanish tapas dishes, such as olives, stuffed vine leaves, almonds, grilled octopus and spicy sausage.

NOTES

....

....

....

....